DAWGS

Center Point
Large Print

**This Large Print Book carries the
Seal of Approval of N.A.V.H.**

DAWGS

A True Story of Lost Animals and the Kids Who Rescued Them

DIANE TRULL
with Meredith Wargo

CENTER POINT LARGE PRINT
THORNDIKE, MAINE

This Center Point Large Print edition
is published in the year 2020 by arrangement with
Kensington Publishing Corp.

The text of this Large Print edition is unabridged.
In other aspects, this book may vary
from the original edition.
Printed in the United States of America
on permanent paper.
Set in 16-point Times New Roman type.

ISBN: 978-1-64358-593-2

The Library of Congress has cataloged this record
under Library of Congress Control Number: 2020930518

*This book is dedicated
to those who make a difference*

*One animal at a time...
One child at a time...
One day at a time...*

Contents

PART THREE

DAWGS

DAWGS' Mission Statement

WE ARE CHILDREN AND ADULT volunteers who care deeply about animals and our community.

We want children in our program to learn responsibility, commitment, and a sense of caring for animals and community service.

We want to create an awareness within our community about the immediate need to reduce the number of unwanted and discarded animals. The cornerstone of our program is to educate and promote the concept of spaying and neutering.

We want to make sure every animal can find its way home. If it can't find its way home, then we will provide a safe, caring, and secure environment until it finds a new home. We strongly believe that every dog deserves the opportunity to live its life as part of a loving and caring family. All dogs are equal in our eyes, and each one has a special gift to give.

We believe that a caring and compassionate commitment to the animals that we share our lives with will provide for an enriching environment for us all.

We believe that it is our responsibility to leave the footprints for the ones that will come behind us, to make a difference and to make our contributions meaningful and long-lasting.

We are making a difference. Will you?

PART ONE

Some people talk to animals. Not many listen though. That's the problem.

—*A. A. MILNE,*
Winnie-the-Pooh

CHAPTER 1

Out of the Mouths of Babes

■ ■ ■ ■ ■

Photo by Diane Trull

SPENCER

Spencer was a six-year-old cocker spaniel when he was dropped off at the shelter after his owner passed away. Spencer was grieving and refused to eat. Each day, he would stand in the corner and whine for hours. All the volunteers and workers made a point of visiting him, but nothing seemed to help. His kennel was filled with toys and stuffed animals and they all remained untouched. He was miserable.

One day, two-year-old Sophia and her parents

stopped by the sanctuary. Sophia went straight to Spencer's pen and started talking to him, as only a child can. Spencer stopped whining immediately and went over and licked her face, which set off a chain of giggles from Sophia. She handed Spencer some doggie treats, which he gently took from her hand. As long as Sophia was near, Spencer was content and happy.

Sophia and her parents adopted Spencer, ensuring that Sophia and Spencer could continue snuggling and playing together for a lifetime.

■ ■ ■ ■ ■

EVERYBODY'S LIFE HAS ITS FAIR SHARE of defining moments. Moments so unique they completely transform your world. I was an elementary school teacher, so you would think I'd be better prepared for those pivotal turning points. But what I've learned over time is, when you're facing a truth that invites you to change the way you live, you have to make a decision. And regardless of the choice you make, your life will never be the same.

One of my life-changing moments happened in March 2003. It was Tuesday morning at Allyn Finch Intermediate School where I taught fourth-grade reading. And like every Tuesday, my students were sitting in four small groups scattered around the room, each under a different Harry Potter house crest banner that had been made from felt and suspended from the ceiling. The children were reading out loud to each other from our local newspaper, the *Dalhart Daily Texan*. The smell of glue and construction paper filled the classroom from the students' just completed spring art projects.

Early in my career I learned the value of multitasking while I taught. As I was working one-on-one with Mitchell, who was reading out loud to me at my desk, I couldn't help but notice that a small group of girls sitting near the front of the classroom wasn't participating in the assignment. Instead, the trio was leaning over their desks looking at a photograph in the newspaper. Their small heads were huddled together, a mixture of brown and blond. I decided to wait a few more minutes before saying anything to them when they stood up and started walking toward me, newspaper in hand.

"Mrs. Trull, may we interrupt you for a minute?" Ally politely asked as Kali and Cortney stood by her side.

"Of course," I said. "Do you have a question about the assignment?"

"No," she said, laying out the newspaper across my desk. "We found this picture of all these dogs and puppies in the paper and we want to know what's going to happen to them."

An adult reading the paper would have probably overlooked the image. After all, a black-

and-white photo of a crudely taped cardboard box overflowing with puppies was hardly newsworthy. But the mishmash of fuzzy round heads and fat little paws poking out in every direction from the puppy pile had drawn the girls in like a magnet.

"Well," I said, pausing for a minute. "These dogs don't currently have a home. Dalhart has a facility where lost animals stay until they can find a new home."

"The caption under the photo says the dogs are available for adoption and that anybody interested in getting one should call the animal control office before Friday," Kali added. "But what happens to the dogs after Friday?"

I didn't know what to say and I certainly didn't want to teach an unplanned lesson about the sobering reality of animal homelessness. So instead I encouraged them to ask their parents about adopting a dog, which would help reduce the animal overpopulation problem.

Satisfied with my answer, the girls went back to their desks and Mitchell started reading out loud to me again. But after a few minutes, Mitchell stopped when the girls reappeared.

"Mrs. Trull, we have some more questions," Cortney said. "Where were these puppies found and who's taking care of them?"

"Well, they were probably found somewhere around town," I said. "And the people who work at the animal control facility where the dogs are staying now are taking care of them. Why don't you go back to your desk and finish your reading assignment? We don't have much time left before lunch." I was trying to deftly divert their attention off the dogs.

As they walked away, Mitchell once again started reading to me. But before he could finish the paragraph that he had started, he informed me that the girls were heading back.

"Here they come again," he said, slightly exasperated.

"These dogs are all so cute," Kali continued as she held out the newspaper. "What happens if nobody takes them home?"

I've always encouraged my students to ask questions about things they don't understand. But as I listened to their confusion and concern about the puppies, I was at a loss for words.

Animals have always been an important part of my life. My husband, Mark, and I were forever rescuing stray dogs and cats, making them our pets or finding them new homes. And even though I did my small part to help when I could, I was painfully aware, like most other animal lovers, of the overwhelming problem of homeless animals.

As a result, my struggle right then was real. Should I risk telling my students the truth about stray animals or should I assure them that the dogs would be adopted, even though I knew they probably wouldn't be? As much as I hated being the bearer of bad news, I realized I had no other choice.

"All across the country, there's a problem with animal overpopulation," I began. "Unfortunately, we have the same problem here in Dalhart. There are too many cats and dogs compared to the number of families that want pets. Instead of allowing the animals to run loose and become sick or injured, animal shelters are safe places where they can stay and see if somebody will adopt them and give them a new home."

The girls nodded their heads, following my seemingly sage and adult logic.

"But most of the shelters are so overcrowded the animals can only stay for a short time," I continued. "If nobody adopts them within a few days, then, sadly, they are put to sleep."

I cringed a little as I said those last three words. I am an animal advocate, and it bothers me that such a nice little term is used to describe something so ugly.

The group became very still when my words sunk in. Nobody said anything for several seconds. The incomprehension of this heinous crime showed on their young faces.

Kali's green eyes widened in disbelief, and she broke the silence. "So you mean the dogs are killed just because they don't have somebody to care for them?"

"How can that be right?" Cortney challenged. "People shouldn't be able to do that to them. It's not the dogs' fault that they don't have homes."

When you're nine years old, it's hard to understand that atrocities happen in the real world. It's even harder to accept that they can happen in your own backyard.

Ally remained quiet as she continued staring at the photograph. I was afraid she was going to start crying. But she didn't. Instead, she glanced at her classmates, took a deep breath, held it a moment, then exhaled.

"What is it, Ally?" Cortney asked.

Ally turned the newspaper around so it was right-side up for us. She slowly tapped the picture with her small index finger. "I don't want any of these dogs to die." She spoke softly, almost in a whisper. "Isn't there something we can do to save them?"

The question hung in the air like chalk dust floating across a ray of sunshine. It wasn't what I had expected her to say and I hesitated with my response. The needless killing of healthy or treatable shelter animals has always been an issue for me. What should I tell the kids when the truth was so heartbreaking?

"It's not okay to kill healthy dogs just because they don't have a home to go to," I finally said.

"Unfortunately, this is how our society deals with the overwhelming problem of pet overpopulation. But it's not a good solution. You say you want to do something to help the animals and I will support you in any way I can. Each of you has the ability to make a difference if this is something you really believe in."

As a schoolteacher, I was required to follow structured lesson plans, but my personal passion has always been to inspire and encourage young children to strive for greatness and to live to their fullest potential. I knew my fourth-grade class was a compassionate bunch, and I knew the girls' concern for the homeless animals was genuine.

It took Ally's simple and heartfelt plea to set the wheels in motion. Over the next several days, I talked to the entire class about what we could do to help the dogs. A lot of my students were deeply troubled by the thought of any innocent animal being put down. They were not content to leave the fate of these unwanted dogs to the city. They wanted to turn their concern into action.

Looking back, I'm still not sure which one of my students suggested starting our own animal sanctuary. At the time, it was nothing more than one of several ideas innocently tossed out. But once spoken, this particular spark lit the imagination of most of my students and quickly turned into a flame that took on a life of its own.

Later that evening, I was having dinner with

22

Mark, as well as our son, Tyler, who was a junior in high school, and our daughter, Katie, who was attending college in Kansas but was home visiting for a few days. One of the most important lessons I'd learned as a teacher was to seek my family's counsel regarding some of my class projects to make sure I wasn't biting off more than I could chew. I told them about my students' desire to start an animal shelter to save the city's homeless dogs.

"Do you think it's a crazy idea?" I asked them.

"Not at all," Mark said. "I think this will be a great activity for the kids. It will be an opportunity to teach them about compassion, empathy, and giving back to the community. These are great life skills that they can use, and, at the same time, they'll be helping to save animals. And really how many dogs can there be?"

Little did we realize how that innocent question would change our world forever.

The next day at school I told my excited students that we were moving forward with starting our own animal shelter.

"Somehow, someway, we've got to have our own place so we can start helping all of these poor dogs," Cortney said. She was a soft-spoken girl with a shy smile, and she wore her emotions on her sleeve. I knew she would do anything to help these animals have a better life.

"I know we can make our shelter really special," Kali added. She smiled, and a tiny dimple formed at the corner of her mouth. "There's no way we're going to let anything bad happen to any of the dogs we save."

It was obvious that my students weren't going to settle for anything less than helping as many animals as quickly as possible. And although I didn't realize right then the complete impact they would have, I did have a feeling that their heartfelt efforts would result in something important.

CHAPTER 2
Innocent Beginnings

■ ■ ■ ■ ■

Photo by Diane Trull

ROMEO

Romeo was a little Lhasa apso that we found cowering in a kennel at the Amarillo animal control facility. He was so badly matted the agent who picked him up couldn't determine if the dog was male or female. The dog could barely walk and the fur on his face was so thick he couldn't see.

After we rescued Romeo, we took him to a local groomer. It took more than six hours to remove the years of matted fur and debris. Once he was cleaned up, we discovered that his right eye was seriously infected. We immediately took him to our veterinarian who prescribed creams and antibiotics. As Romeo's eye became worse, the vet advised us to remove it because it was causing Romeo a lot of pain. Although Romeo had a difficult time with the surgery, he quickly recovered and was ready to go to our adoption events.

A family with two small children saw him as we entered the door and knew he needed to be a part of their lives.

Today, Romeo is greatly loved and very happy.

■ ■ ■ ■ ■

I ONCE READ THAT AGNES DE MILLE, an American dancer and choreographer, said that no trumpets sound when the important decisions of our life are made; rather, destiny is made known silently. Who could have imagined that a photograph of some homeless puppies would be a catalyst for causing so much commotion and change?

After we officially decided to start our own animal shelter, it became the main topic of conversation in my classroom. Every day it was the only thing my students wanted to talk about. In their innocent minds, all they wanted to do was save as many dogs as possible. They weren't as concerned with the logistics of how to make that happen.

One afternoon after school, several of my students were helping me swap out the display on my bulletin board when the topic once again turned to rescuing animals.

"It's so unfair that a dog might die just because it stays at the pound too long," Alix stated as she pulled off the trim around the bulletin board. One of my twenty-five students, she loved animals and was excited at the prospect of saving some of the city's dogs. "We've got to figure out some way to help them right away."

"Do you think they're scared being locked up in a strange place?" Kali asked. A concerned look spread across her face as she waited for my answer.

Before I could even think of a response, Molly burst into the classroom, visibly upset. While I knew that almost all children loved animals, Molly's interest was keener than most. She had been a student of mine for the past seven months, and the entire time she had talked about wanting a dog of her own. I think everybody in our school knew how badly she wanted one.

"There you are!" she exclaimed. "I've been looking all over for you."

I wasn't sure if she was speaking to me or to her classmates, but she had our full attention.

"You're not going to believe what I just heard," she continued. "It's really terrible. Sadye and Sarah told me that the people at the pound sometimes take the dogs that don't get adopted out to the shooting range and shoot them instead of putting them to sleep. Do you think that's really true? How could anybody do such a horrible thing?"

I had heard rumors that the shelter animals were sometimes used as target practice by those in law enforcement and security at the prison, but I didn't want to believe it. Not in this day and age, and certainly not in our town.

"I don't know if that's true or not," I said to my anxious group. "Unfortunately, there are a lot of bad things that happen in the world, even here in Dalhart. What I do know, however, is that we should focus on the positive. If you are serious about starting an animal shelter, then let's put all of our energy into that and see what good things we can make happen."

It was in that moment when everybody's desire to help the dogs really escalated.

The next day in class, I outlined what we would need to do to turn their idea into a reality. "I think your plan of starting an animal shelter is a good one, but before we begin, we'll have to get approval from the school and from the Dalhart City Council."

After school was out, I approached our principal about the students' idea. Although she was supportive of the project, she asked me to run it by the other teachers to make sure they were also onboard. Unfortunately, none of my colleagues shared our enthusiasm about rescuing the dogs, while several went as far as saying it was a terrible idea. Although I was surprised by their response, I wasn't going to let it deter our plans. Instead, I started preparing for our presentation to the city council the very next day. Since none of the children had ever been inside the council chambers, this would be a great teaching moment for them to learn how a city government operates.

"We'll have to write a proposal that spells out our plan for how we will rescue the dogs from the city pound," I explained. "We'll also have to figure out how we're going to raise money so we can care for the animals once we get them."

The next few weeks were busy. We studied how local governments work and explored their powers and responsibilities. We also learned about the functions of city councils and how they are structured. We drafted and submitted a formal request asking to be placed on the agenda at the next Dalhart City Council meeting, which was scheduled for April 9, 2003. We polished our proposal to the city, which outlined our plans for starting an animal sanctuary and rehearsed what we were going to say. I wanted to be sure my students were well prepared for the meeting.

Finally, the evening of our presentation arrived. Mark and I and twenty-eight anxious nine-year-old students stood in the lobby waiting for the meeting to start. I could tell everyone was very apprehensive. Practicing in a classroom in front of your peers is a little different from speaking in front of complete strangers. Luckily, we were first on the agenda, so we didn't have to wait long.

"Just remember to speak from your heart and be respectful of each of the council members," I said as I gave each child an encouraging hug. I was hoping they couldn't see that I was as nervous as they were.

One by one, the children took turns at the microphone explaining their idea.

"There seems to be a lot of people who decide they want a dog, but when things don't work out for some reason, they give their dog to the pound. Or, if they get tired of taking care of their pet, some people just turn it loose, which is worse."

"Dogs have feelings just like us and each one has a special gift to give. How can it be right to kill them if the only thing they want is someone to love but they don't have anybody to care for them? We don't do that to homeless people, do we?"

"Our plan is really simple. Instead of killing the dogs that don't get adopted at your place, give them to us. We don't care if they're blind, deaf, old or sick. We don't care if they're big or small. We don't even care if they have three legs or four. We'll take good care of them until we can find new homes for them. And although we know we can't solve all pet problems with our rescue, it's a step. We want to start our very own no-kill animal sanctuary right here in Dalhart."

Their eager faces looked expectantly across the room at the council members. The members' reactions seemed to be mixed and I realized this was probably the first time a group of children had ever made a formal request.

The Dalhart city manager was the first to speak up. "With all due respect, we appreciate the fact that you want to help these animals, but I'm not sure you understand how much work is involved in caring for them." He smiled despairingly. "They require a lot of attention every single day, and since you're in school most days, you won't have much time to help out. There have been several adults who have tried to help our town's homeless dogs before and they didn't have much luck. Truthfully, I'm not convinced that you're going to be able to make that much of a difference."

I couldn't hold myself back any longer; I stood up and said, "And also with all due respect, Members of the Council, I don't think you realize that my students have passion and desire and a sense of responsibility that many adults are lacking," I said. "Look at their faces. These children still believe in the greater good. If you tell them they can't do this, you might as well tell them their dreams aren't worth chasing. I know what my students are capable of when they put their minds to something. Give them a chance and see what they can do. I have no doubt you'll be surprised at the outcome."

My heart pounded wildly as I listened to the council members openly debate the pros and cons of the children's proposal. They seemed to be equally divided in their viewpoints. After what seemed like an eternity, one of the council members called for a vote. By a slim margin, the city council agreed to release some of Dalhart's lost dogs to us. They also voted to provide one thousand dollars in materials and a monthly stipend of two hundred and fifty dollars to help us with the cost of caring for the animals. The money allotted to our efforts would come from the city's animal control budget.

The smack of the gavel by the Dalhart mayor made everything official. I let out a breath I hadn't realized I had been holding.

"We did it, Mrs. Trull! We're really going to save some dogs!" The kids cheered as they danced and hopped around the podium.

"Everybody did such a great job," I said. "I'm so very proud of each of you."

I gently gathered the children together and guided them toward the door, but before leaving the room, I glanced over my shoulder at the council members. They were talking among themselves and I could see uncertainty on most of their faces. I couldn't help but wonder if they were just placating the children with their decision. I'm sure they thought that the kids' commitment would only last a few weeks and this pet project would then go away. But knowing how passionate my students were about helping the dogs, I knew better than to bet against them.

The next morning the buzz was palpable in my classroom. The thrill of what had happened the previous night lingered in the air. I decided to give the kids a few minutes to settle down before starting the day's reading lesson. Listening to their excitement, I went to the chalkboard and wrote in big letters, "Don't ever, ever give up on what you believe in."

With all the commotion in the room, none of us noticed when the city's animal control officer appeared. Dressed in a chocolate-brown uniform and spinning a straw cowboy hat in his hands, the officer stood in the doorway and announced in a loud voice that he had a dozen dogs out in his truck. A large wad of chewing tobacco was wedged inside his bottom lip.

"Where do y'all want them?" he asked nobody in particular. He used the back of his hand to wipe away the spit that had dribbled down his chin.

The giggling and chatting in the room came to a halt. I pushed back from my desk and slowly walked toward our unexpected visitor. "I think there must be some sort of misunderstanding, Officer," I said, trying to keep my voice level. "The decision was made only last night to let us have some of the dogs from the city pound. We had no idea that any of the dogs would be released to us so soon. As you can imagine, we don't have a place to keep them yet."

"Well, aren't you the ones who get these unwanted mutts from now on?" He glanced around the classroom. "Do you want me to bring them in here with the kids? If not, I'll take them to be killed."

I needed to stay calm for the sake of my students, so I asked if he would give us until the end of the day to come up with a plan. All the while my mind was reeling, trying to comprehend how the city could possibly have that many stray dogs at one time.

"Yep, I can hang on to them until later this afternoon," the officer agreed. "But if you change your mind about wanting them, just let me know. It really doesn't matter either way." Before he turned to walk out, he settled his hat on his head and took one final look around the room.

Alicia, another one of my students who was anxious to get our class project off the ground, stood up from her desk. "Excuse me, sir," she said respectfully. "Just so you know, we won't be changing our minds. We want the dogs in your truck. Please bring every single one of them back to us this afternoon."

Alicia and her younger brother, Jesse, who was in the third grade, had moved to Dalhart from Kansas after the academic year had started. As was true for many children who move in the middle of a school year, it can take some time to settle in. I was proud of Alicia and her newfound confidence which had inspired her to speak up in front of her classmates, many of whom she didn't know all that well. The class was very proud of her, too, as they all clapped and cheered.

Somehow, by the time school was over, several students had convinced their parents to temporarily adopt the first batch of five dogs. Darla, an aide at the school (and an animal lover), took the seven puppies home to her house. But little did we realize that the floodgates were about to break open.

Now that the city was releasing dogs to us, we had a pressing problem. I panicked a bit when I realized that we hadn't completely thought through the logistics of what we were about to embark upon. Where were we going to keep all the incoming animals? Foster families were a good temporary solution, but we needed something permanent, and soon.

Because, like clockwork, the animal control officer showed up to my classroom every day, dropping off more and more dogs.

CHAPTER 3

Little Hands, Big Hearts

■ ■ ■ ■ ■

Photo by Diane Trull

SCRUFFY

Scruffy was a darling terrier with the kindest eyes.

During a terrible Dalhart snowstorm, a compassionate woman named Jean found a dog freezing in the cold. She took him in, warmed him up, fed him a nice meal, and named him Scruffy. Then she called us for help. Fortunately, one of our foster homes had an opening and could take the dog.

When Jean dropped Scruffy off, she also

dropped off a care package she had prepared for him. She asked that we let her know when he was adopted.

We took Scruffy to our adoption events for several weeks, but he never found the right family. We decided to feature him on "Studio 4," Amarillo's only lifestyle and entertainment show, and that's when we got a call from Jean. She had never forgotten Scruffy and was so worried about him.

After seeing him again on the show, Jean decided he needed to be part of her family. Scruffy, normally a shy dog, literally jumped for joy when Jean came to pick him up. He is now in his forever home.

■ ■ ■ ■ ■

LIVING IN A SMALL TOWN is similar to living in a fishbowl. Your business can quickly become everybody else's business. And depending on what your business is, that can be good or bad. So, when a local justice of the peace contacted me at school one day, I knew word was spreading about our grassroots efforts.

The judge had been in the audience the week before when we made our presentation to the city council. She owned a half-acre lot in town, on which she had built a three-car garage, a chicken coop, and a vegetable garden. Because the judge also shared our concern for the town's homeless dog problem, she offered to donate her entire parcel of land and its structures to us if it would help in saving the strays. An added bonus was that her property shared a fence with the Dalhart Animal Hospital, which would make our visits to the veterinarian easier. Thrilled by her generosity, we were anxious to convert her property into a makeshift shelter.

Every day after school, a small army of students changed into their work clothes, pulled on their garden gloves, and headed over to the judge's property. After spending hours in the classroom, they willingly gave up their afternoons to create the sanctuary. And every evening, I would drive the kids back to their homes.

Over the course of a week, the children cleared out the garage and swept it spotless. They raked the yard and pulled all the weeds. They transformed the chicken coop into a clean and comfortable space that would keep the puppies safe. Even the potholes scattered throughout the alley next to the garage were filled with chicken manure and topsoil so the dogs wouldn't injure themselves as they were walked around the property.

Watching the kids work so hard, I marveled at their dedication. Although they were covered in mud and dirt from head to toe, they weren't whining or complaining. Most children their ages would rather be at home playing video games or, at a minimum, they'd object to doing physical labor. Instead, this group had voluntarily given up their free time to create something they believed in.

And while a core group of students provided the physical labor to create the shelter, other students focused on raising money to fund it. Working with the city, we started a paper-recycling program at all the schools throughout the district to generate ongoing revenue for our cause. We also held several bake sales and car washes. And, of course, we graciously accepted any donation, no matter the amount.

At that time, my husband was working for a company called Premium Standard Farms. When Mark's boss, John, learned of our class project, he arranged for their company to contribute to our cause. With their donation, we purchased wire hog panels and metal stakes from Gebo's, our local hardware store. I recruited Mark, who was a master at do-it-yourself projects, to build a few kennels around the property. Naïvely, he and I thought we would have to put up only a dozen or so runs to accommodate all the dogs. But looking back, I don't think we've stopped building kennels since that first day.

Once all the runs were set up, we moved the first of our four-legged residents from all our foster families into their new haven. One month after deciding we wanted to save Dalhart's animals, our little shelter was officially open for business!

Now that we had a physical location, it didn't take long for the children to establish a routine. After school, I would shuttle the kids to the shelter. Once they arrived, everybody swung into action caring for the dogs. And there were always plenty of chores to go around. The kids went from kennel to kennel, feeding the dogs and cleaning their pens. They scrubbed the water buckets and dragged garden hoses around to refill them with fresh water. They took the dogs for walks throughout the neighborhood and played with them in their pens. But, most important, they called the animals by name and could tell stories about each one of them, just as if they were family pets. Every dog in our shelter had a name. It may not have been the same name from child to child, but every dog had a name.

One of the local television stations ran a news story about what we were trying to accomplish. When one of the animal rescue groups in Amarillo saw the story, they invited us to participate in their weekend adoption programs at the PetSmart store in Amarillo. We knew the best way for our dogs to find a new home was to move them out of Dalhart. Readopting them within the city limits would not solve the city's rampant animal homeless problem. Amarillo could potentially be a great adoption solution for us.

The following Saturday we started what became our weekend ritual. We loaded several of the dogs into the back of my white Suburban and made the hour-long drive to Amarillo. The kids stood patiently for hours in the Pet Smart parking lot, each holding the leash of the dog he or she was responsible for. They eagerly talked about our dogs to the people coming into the store, in the hopes of finding them a new home. Before heading back to Dalhart at the end of the day, we stopped and bought hamburgers and french fries for everybody, which also became a tradition. For the few dogs that weren't lucky enough to get adopted and were returning to the shelter with us, the kids made sure to share their dinner with them.

In June, the council invited us to make a presentation at their next meeting. Foolishly, we assumed it was to update them on our progress. Although they gave us only twenty-four hours' notice, we worked hard to be ready for the meeting. Since opening our doors, we had taken in thirty-two dogs of every breed, size, and health condition imaginable, which enabled us to have some great stories to share.

"Can we bring some of the puppies with us to the meeting, Mrs. Trull?" Molly asked. "The council members might like to see some of the dogs we've saved." She was always promoting our rescues to anybody who would listen.

"I think that's a great idea," I said. "And I think we should also tell them the starfish story."

In Texas, all schoolchildren are required to take aptitude tests. The focus of the fourth-grade exam is on reading. The children read paragraph stories and answer questions about them, testing their comprehension. My students had recently read the starfish story as part of their exam and all had commented on how much what they did was like the boy in the story.

The next night, Mark and I walked into the meeting with thirty-five students and two golden retriever puppies at our sides. I was glad to see that only a handful of people were in attendance. I don't like being in the limelight, and I knew some of the kids might have gotten nervous if there had been a large turnout. Standing at the podium, I quickly scanned the room, took a deep breath and began.

"Tonight, we'd like to share one of our favorite stories with you," I said, motioning Alix over to the microphone.

After I introduced her to the group, Alix began reading from the piece of paper that she was holding. Her little body was shaking because she was so nervous. I gently put my hand on her shoulder.

"There are many versions of this story, but our favorite one is about a man walking down the beach after a terrible thunderstorm," Alix began.

"He sees a young boy frantically throwing starfish stranded on the beach back into the sea as fast as he can. The beach is littered with thousands of these poor creatures. The man walks up to the young boy, shakes his head, and says, 'Son, why are you doing this? Look at this beach! You can't save all these starfish. You can't possibly make a difference.' Without stopping, the boy bends down, picks up another starfish, and hurls it as far as he can into the ocean. Then he looks up at the man and replies, 'But sir, I made a difference to that one!' "

"The moral is that anybody can make a difference," I said when Alix finished. "My students love this story and what it represents. That's how we came up with our motto for the shelter. 'Making a difference one animal at a time, one child at a time, one day at a time.' We believe it sums up what we're trying to accomplish in rescuing the homeless dogs of our community.

"During the first few days of our operation, when we were trying to figure out what we were doing, most of the help came from a dedicated core group of students in my fourth-grade class. But as we became more organized and received more dogs, the number rose to more than one hundred students who volunteer on a regular basis. Considering that Allyn Finch Intermediate School has a student body of two hundred and fifty, I think that's a pretty impressive commitment.

"Now, I'd like to turn the presentation over to some of our volunteers, who will tell you about some of the special dogs we've rescued. I can't tell you how proud I am of what this group of children has accomplished in a short period of time. They have shown a level of caring and commitment to animals that should inspire everyone."

Jesse stepped up to the microphone holding a poster board that had several pictures of a dog named Hooch glued to it. The one-year-old pit bull had been used as a bait-dog in a dogfighting ring.

"Hooch was one of the very first dogs we rescued," Jesse began. "You would think Hooch would be really mean, but he's not. He's super-sweet and loves everyone. When he first came to the shelter, he was super-skinny and had wounds all over him. He had terrible cuts on his mouth and nose, but he's completely healed now. He loves to get treats and will patiently wait his turn for them. Thank you for helping us save Hooch. Thank you for helping us make a difference."

Jesse handed the microphone to Alix, who stepped forward and held up a large color photo of a beautiful golden-colored dog. "This is Cheyenne, a chow chow and shepherd mix. She's had a hard life. Her owner gave her to us after she gave birth to eight really cute puppies. When we first got her, Cheyenne was really sick and needed a lot of bed rest. She was also very sad. But then she met Hooch and they became best friends. They are totally inseparable and when they walk around, their tails are always wrapped around each other.

"Today, she is a happy dog. Thank you for helping us save Cheyenne and all of her puppies. Thank you for helping us make a difference."

Alix continued to hold the microphone while Molly showed two photos of Shaggy, a ten-year-old chow with an ugly scar on his back.

"Shaggy was really pitiful when he first came to the shelter, but we took extra special care of him," Molly said. "He probably thinks his full name is 'Poor Shaggy' because that's what we're always saying when we're around him. But we love him and think he's pretty cool. Thank you for helping us save Shaggy. Thank you for helping us make a difference."

"Thank you for helping us make a big difference in all these animals' lives!" the kids jointly exclaimed at the end of their presentation. "Our dogs aren't mangy mutts. They are really good dogs that just want to be loved."

The children were beaming as a small round of applause trickled across the room. Alix walked over to the council members and handed the city manager the stack of photos the kids had just held up.

"Well, that's all good and well, but what do you want me to do with these?" the city manager asked rather brusquely as he tossed the photos on the table.

"Oh, we'll take them back," I said, hurrying over to reclaim the photos. I was a little surprised by the tone of his voice.

"Well, there is no doubt that you are to be commended for all your hard work," one of the council members remarked. "But as touching as your presentation is, there are three problems. First, we've been getting quite a few complaints from folks living in the neighborhood who say that the barking is getting out of control. One of my friends has a ninety-year-old mother who can't sleep at night because of all the noise. I went by the facility the other day and when I poked my head over the fence, the dogs started barking and didn't stop until I left. Secondly, there is a terrible smell coming from the shelter, and the neighbors aren't happy about that either, especially on windy days. And last, but not least, we've discovered that Dalhart has a zoning ordinance that states a facility such as yours must be located at least one hundred feet from any residence, church, school, or hospital. Right now, because your shelter sits in the middle of a residential area, you are in violation of that ordinance."

46

The silence in the room was sudden and intense. This was our first inkling that there were any issues with what we were doing. I looked at Mark and he took my hand; he obviously was catching on faster than I was. My mind was trying to process all the councilman's objections, but his comment about the smell emanating from our shelter threw me. The animal hospital adjacent to our shelter had several outdoor pens for holding horses, cattle, and other farm animals—sometimes for extended periods—when they were receiving medical treatment. Next to the pens and pushed up against the fence that divided the judge's property from the clinic was a pile of manure six feet tall, ten feet deep, and at least fifteen feet long. The manure had been there for years without any complaints. Yet, somebody was now claiming that a handful of dogs was causing the stench?

It was a sad moment because the kids were so proud of their accomplishments. Confused, they looked at me from across the platform.

One of the little girls in our group, Eureka, didn't understand the significance of what had just been said. Before I could make my way across the room to address the council members, she picked up the microphone in her little hands.

"Why do you want to hurt our dogs?" Eureka asked in a small, broken voice. Even with the microphone, her voice came across as a whisper.

Although the councilman showed no emotion after Eureka's accusation, his reply sounded defiant.

"I don't want to hurt the dogs," he said. "I don't really care about them one way or the other. What I do care about, though, is making sure that people like this man's mother can get plenty of sleep."

"Well, can't she just turn off her hearing aids when she goes to sleep?" Eureka asked. "I bet she wouldn't hear the dogs barking then."

To a nine-year-old, turning off somebody's hearing aids seemed like a reasonable solution. But most of the council members didn't agree.

By the end of the meeting, the city council unanimously voted that our shelter had to move. Mark gathered together our teary-eyed delegation of kids and hurried them out of the room. They were crushed by the verdict and were struggling to hold back their emotions.

Stunned by the turn of events, I lingered behind, hoping to challenge the council's decision. But before I could confront them, the city's chief of maintenance quietly pulled me aside.

"Are you aware that the city owns some vacant land on the outskirts of town?" he asked. "It used to be the local processing and slaughter facility during the Depression. There's about two acres of property and several dilapidated buildings, but the site's been vacant since the 1930s. Because it's located next to the shooting range and the cemetery, some of the locals think the place is haunted. It may not be the best solution, but, if you want it for your shelter, I'm sure something can be worked out with the city."

"Since I'm not aware of any other options, I'll go take a look at it," I said, sounding more hopeful than I felt. "Thank you."

Reluctantly, Mark and I drove out to the former slaughterhouse the next day after school. I knew how heartbroken my students would be if they couldn't continue their mission of caring for the dogs. As we parked the truck, we looked across the dilapidated property dotted with dead, twisted trees. I tried to imagine how we could possibly salvage it. The main building sagged in an area choked with weeds and roots and fallen leaves, its white paint faded and flaking. What windows remained were blank gray spaces, giving the place an eerie look. We were warned that the site had no electricity, and the limited water came from an abandoned water well.

This place is a total disaster, I thought, and Mark echoed my feelings.

I stood in front of the broken-down site, my thoughts chasing each other in circles. I didn't like what I saw, but I didn't see that we had any other choice. My students were determined to have a shelter, and the dogs had to move. There was simply no other alternative.

Despite the irony of opening a sanctuary dedicated to affirming life on what was once a killing field where innocent animals were led to slaughter, we made the decision to relocate.

"It's going to take a lot of work, but there will be more space for the dogs and the children and it's not by a busy road," Mark said, looking for the positive.

And with his comment, we started planning what we needed to do.

The next morning, I broke the news to my class about the new location. I admired their steadfast commitment to continuing their mission, no matter the obstacles.

"It's okay, Mrs. Trull," Alix said, speaking for the group. "We aren't afraid to move out there. A few old buildings aren't going to scare us. The dogs need our help and it's up to us to save them."

Within the week, we had an agreement with Dalhart's city officials. The city would loan us the former slaughterhouse property free of charge if we relocated our shelter from the judge's property to this location. In a good faith effort to help the kids, the city also sent out a work crew and a bulldozer to clean up the site. They pushed eighty years of garbage, weeds, and junk into a big pile in the middle of the property and set it on fire. It took three days for the bonfire to burn down.

Once the debris and rubble were gone, the area underwent a total transformation. Neighbors showed up with cans of paint and spruced up the buildings. Moms went door-to-door collecting donations. Dads repaired the broken windows and the rickety fence. Local veterinarians offered their services free of charge. The Mormon missionaries came out on their free days and helped in a variety of ways. They were a great role model for the children. Another news story ran about what we were trying to accomplish, and before the story had finished airing, I had a phone call from Garth Merrick, owner of Merrick Pet Care, Inc. Founded in Hereford, Texas, in 1988, Merrick was a leader in natural and organic pet food. Garth graciously offered to donate dog food to us. I was touched and thrilled by his benevolence.

All the community support reinforced that a lot of wonderful people who truly love animals are out there. I was extremely hopeful for the future of our shelter.

Both of my own children also got in on the action. Katie and Tyler grabbed hammers and nails and recruited their friends to build dog pens throughout the property. But when they were constructing the kennels inside the red barn, they made a gruesome discovery—multiple dog carcasses were piled on top of one another. Even more disturbing, many of the bodies still had collars with dog tags. Since we had already suspected that some of the homeless dogs were being used for target practice at the shooting range next door, we assumed their bodies were simply dumped on the abandoned slaughterhouse property instead of being properly buried. The fact that several of the animals were wearing collars and tags probably meant that not much effort was made in trying to reunite Dalhart's lost pets with their owners. We made sure these poor dogs finally had a proper burial.

The day before we were planning to relocate the dogs from the judge's property to our new location, I had a visit from three well-dressed, middle-aged women. By the look of their clothing, I assumed they weren't intending to offer their help in getting us moved. They introduced themselves as concerned, church-going citizens.

Although I was a bit baffled by their announcement, I asked them what I ask everybody who comes to the shelter. "Are you interested in adopting a dog?"

"Oh goodness, no," replied one of the women. She seemed repulsed by my question. "We're here today because we'd like to pray for you."

"Excuse me?" I said, thinking they must have me confused with somebody else. Having moved from Missouri to Dalhart in 1998, Mark and I were aware of the town's religious fervor.

The city has dozens of churches of every denomination in its four-square miles. We were regular church-goers ourselves. But never had anybody offered to save my soul.

"We represent a larger group of local citizens who believe that you are misguided in what you're trying to do," another lady in the group said in a matter-of-fact tone. "It's evil to save animals that people have cast aside. You shouldn't be teaching innocent children that the lives of animals are valuable. Dogs don't have souls. It's a waste of precious time that could be used on something more meaningful and charitable."

I couldn't believe what I was hearing. I gathered my jumbled thoughts for a moment, then said, "Well, my husband and I don't see it that way. We are teaching children the importance of empathy, responsibility, teamwork, and generosity. We are teaching them how to give back to their community. We are encouraging them to be the change they want to see in the world. The dogs that we're saving are innocent victims and deserve a better life. I'm sorry if you don't agree with that, but we're not doing anything wrong."

As politely as I could, I thanked them for stopping by and started to escort them off the property. There was still a lot of work to be done before the move and I didn't have time to debate the morals of our motives. As they were leaving, one of the ladies turned to me and asked if I would join them in a prayer. I assured her I was happy to participate and right before the group said their final amen, I quickly added "And please bless all the children and the dogs in their care."

After weeks of preparation, hard work, and a few sore muscles, on June 18, 2003, we officially opened the Dalhart Animal Wellness Group and Sanctuary—more lovingly known as DAWGS. Although our facilities were somewhat primitive compared to other animal shelters, what we lacked in glamour, we made up in dedication, spirit, and love.

The kids were eager to start moving the dogs into their new home. Jesse and Alix were concerned about the pregnant dogs in our care, so it was decided the best place to house the expectant mothers and their soon-to-be litters was in the main building. While cleaning out the space, the kids came across a swallow's nest high in the corner of the building.

"I wonder how the birds got in here?" Jesse asked. "Let's move their nest outside so the dogs won't bother the birds."

Mark had Jesse help him and they gently moved the nest to the other side of the door.

But every day the birds showed up and started rebuilding their nest inside the shelter. And every day the partially built nest was moved outside.

"I guess the birds are trying to tell us something," Alix finally decided after several days of relocating the nest. "They seem just as determined to build their nest inside as we are about building our shelter and saving dogs. I guess we should just leave them and their nest alone."

Mark acknowledged the wisdom of her words and placed some wire mesh around the nest area to protect the birds from the dogs. Over the next several weeks, we watched as six baby swallows were hatched and lovingly cared for by their parents.

We arrived at the shelter one afternoon and found the family of eight birds lined up on the ledge over the door. They looked at us when we walked in and then flew off together. We never saw them again. I can't help but feel that they were waiting to see us one last time to say good-bye. To this day, we still have that nest. It's a wonderful reminder of commitment, persistence, and what we're trying to accomplish.

CHAPTER 4

Dalhart's Roots

■ ■ ■ ■ ■

Photo by Diane Trull

PRINCESS MITZY

We received a call regarding a little Pekinese that was found in a local animal control facility. She was a pitiful sight, with major infections over her entire mouth and body. Her huge brown eyes pleaded for help when we rescued her.

After taking the dog to our local veterinarian, it was determined her overall health was good, but she would need dental surgery. After most of her teeth were removed, it was apparent the dog was a little princess, so the office staff named her Princess Mitzy. When staff members couldn't get her to eat, they offered her small bites of food by hand, which she gratefully accepted. She would then make the most pitiful sounds so she could get more food. Princess Mitzy was adopted by a family with another Pekinese, and both dogs are living the good life.

■ ■ ■ ■ ■

TEXAS IS A STATE of iconic symbols. The Alamo, Longhorn cattle, oil wells, and NASA help paint an image of what life is like here. What doesn't readily come to mind, though, when thinking about the Lone Star State is Dalhart—a dustbowl of a town that sits in the northwestern corner of the Texas Panhandle. Known by many as a gateway to the majestic Colorado Rocky Mountains, Dalhart is usually thought of as a place to pass through rather than as a destination.

But that wasn't always the case. At the turn of the century, Dalhart was a bustling town carving a niche for itself in the history books of the Old West. The town sat in the heart of the historic XIT Ranch—a legendary institution that would impact Dalhart's social mindset.

In the late 1800s, a group of Chicago investors funded the construction of a new state capitol building in Austin. In exchange for payment, the financiers accepted three million acres of uninhabited land in the Texas Panhandle, where they established the XIT Ranch. Stretching across portions of ten Texas counties, XIT became the largest working ranch in the world.

When cattle prices started crashing in the late 1800s, the XIT Ranch crumbled, too. In 1901, the syndicate that owned the ranch started selling off sections of it to pay investors as their bonds came due. Within a few years, most of the land was subdivided and sold to other ranchers and small farmers. The ranch was officially dissolved in 1912 when the last XIT-branded cattle were sold. Today, only a few of the original buildings remain.

As the ranch began to dwindle, settlers who had come to work on the ranch lingered in the area looking for other ways to make a living. Two major railroad lines twisting through town contributed to Dalhart's rapid growth and development. New businesses popped up everywhere, including an assortment of banks, hotels, saloons, and general stores. Dalhart quickly established itself as a center of commerce as the town's population spiked to three thousand five hundred residents. And when oil companies discovered a surplus of oil fields scattered throughout the Panhandle, Dalhart was one of the first towns to sell oil leases.

When the Great Depression started in 1930, Dalhart took a major hit. The town's bank failed on June 27, 1931, a day when the temperature soared to a sweltering 112 degrees. On the heels of the country's worst financial drought, the rains also disappeared, causing a different sort of drought. The Dust Bowl destroyed millions of acres of farmland, and thousands of people living in Texas and Oklahoma were forced to abandon their homes.

But Texans are resilient and many survived the fury of the Great Depression and the Dust Bowl. Families that fled Dalhart in desperation returned years later to help dig the town out from devastation and begin again.

Time hasn't changed much in this close-knit community. Dalhart remains a picture postcard of vintage farmland America. Cattle feedlots envelop the area, tumbleweeds roll aimlessly across the highways, and rows of storefronts in connecting two- and three-story buildings still conduct business along redbrick Denrock Avenue. The addition of dairy farms and a cheese production plant has put Dalhart on the map again as an agribusiness epicenter for Texas, Oklahoma, and New Mexico.

And through it all, the legacy of the XIT Ranch lives on through the XIT Rodeo and Reunion. Since 1937, this annual event has brought thousands of visitors from all over the country into our little backyard. The tradition started as a way to honor the XIT cowboys and the contributions they made to the region. It has since morphed into a three-day celebration with parades, rodeo events, live music, and the biggest draw of all: the world's largest free barbecue.

Most of my students come from multiple-generation Texan stock who scratched out a living from farming or agriculture. The influence of the XIT Ranch remains strong and is never far from the fabric of our daily life. In school, the legacy is woven into the Texas history curriculum. Just north of the US-87 underpass that leads in and out of town, drivers pass the Empty Saddle Monument, a concrete stone statue that commemorates the cowhands and pioneers who died settling the area. And perhaps the most telling influence of XIT is in the attitude of Dalhart's residents—left over from the days of the ranch and perpetuated by generations of farmers—that animals have no rights and are only important for the monetary value they bring at market.

Before our animal shelter, this business-like mentality toward animals often spilled over into how family pets were treated. The concept of dog ownership was very loose. Generally, an animal could live around a particular family's house and be fed, and that animal would be considered their pet. Compounding the problem was that many of the residents felt that the animal overpopulation problem, which was quickly getting out of hand, was somebody else's problem. Stray dogs roaming the streets were an all-too-common sight, to which the standard response was "that's not my dog so it's not my problem." Litters of puppies were frequently born in overgrown fields or abandoned buildings, with little chance of survival. Spaying and neutering were virtually unheard-of practices by most of the locals.

While urban and rural areas throughout the United States face similar overwhelming animal homelessness problems, many Dalhart residents were opting for a solution that was radically different from how other towns were dealing with the situation. Those who had little interest in finding a new home for their pets would often shoot the unwanted animals or turn them loose to fend for themselves among the hundreds of acres of farmland surrounding the city. It was a Wild West atmosphere perpetuated by a community steeped in the agribusiness industry.

But perhaps the most disturbing fact, unbeknownst to most of the residents, including my students and my family, was that Dalhart was destroying more than six hundred homeless dogs every year. A mind-numbing statistic that's even more shocking when you consider that Dalhart's population was only seven thousand people. New York City, the largest city in

America, wasn't even putting down that many animals, per capita, in a year.

How could such an unassuming, docile town have a euthanasia rate six times higher than the national average?

I wonder sometimes, if my students and I had known the ugly truth about the city's rampant history of killing innocent animals and the locals' lax attitudes toward caring for their pets, would we still have gone down this long road of starting our own animal sanctuary? In hindsight, I guess the old saying "what you don't know can't hurt you" was a blessing.

CHAPTER 5

In Sickness and in Health

■ ■ ■ ■ ■

Photos by Diane Trull

SQUIGGLES AND SUPER Y

Squiggles and Super Y were two adorable kittens brought to our sanctuary by a nice family who had found them with their mother. Unfortunately, because of severe health and financial hardships, the family couldn't keep all three cats. They felt the kittens would have a greater chance of being adopted, so they kept the mother and surrendered her babies.

When the kittens were old enough, we took the siblings to our adoption events for two months trying to find a home for them together, as they were inseparable. Unfortunately, most people were interested in only adopting one cat. But Squiggles and Super Y's luck changed when a newlywed couple came to PetSmart with the hope of adding two kittens to their family. As soon as the kittens wrapped their paws around the young couple's fingers, they were in love.

Today, Squiggles and Super Y are living happily in their forever home.

■ ■ ■ ■ ■

A T THE END OF THE DAY, running an animal shelter is no different from running any other type of business. And we soon learned that our modest sanctuary had a lot of expenses.

Although Mark and I were able to personally cover some of the initial costs, we knew we needed a longer-term plan for raising additional funds. But trying to find the time to identify other possible financial sources often took a backseat to the variety of other challenges we were facing.

While we were busy caring for the growing number of dogs that animal control was constantly turning over to us, people started dropping off litters of unwanted kittens at the shelter, often leaving them in flimsy boxes outside the front gate for us to find when we arrived. The accommodations at DAWGS weren't suitable for housing felines, so Mark and I turned our three-car garage at home into a cattery.

Over the years, Mark and I had rescued our fair share of cats that eventually became our family pets. But after discovering that Mark was severely allergic to them, we relocated our indoor cats into the garage, where we built spacious kennels for them to live out their lives in comfort and safety. We also installed heating and air conditioning, so the cats would be comfortable, regardless of the season. Although we hadn't owned cats for several years, it was easy to convert the garage back into a haven for the cats and kittens we were acquiring.

Even though I had grown up with cats and dogs most of my life, I quickly learned that caring for a few family pets was significantly different from caring for a shelter full of rescued animals in varying health and ages. As the school year was winding down, the number of animals in our care was ramping up. We had to constantly adjust our daily routine; we were learning the ropes, from what and when we fed the animals to juggling veterinarian visits for vaccinations, surgeries, and wellness checks.

No sooner had we found our rhythm than we were tested with a new challenge.

It was early August and the sky was nearly cloudless. The scorching days lined up like a company of soldiers waiting their turn for inspection. It was obvious that summer wasn't going on vacation any time soon.

"Mrs. Trull, will you come check on some of the puppies for us?" Molly asked me one morning. It was only nine o'clock and the sun was already too hot.

During the summer months, many of the kids showed up early to get their chores done before the oppressive heat hit. But once the work was done, the kids didn't leave. They usually spent the day hanging out at the shelter and enjoyed play time with many of the dogs.

"Alix and I have been cleaning out the puppy pens because they were such a mess," she said. "I think some of the puppies are really sick. And a lot of them seem to be sleepy and lazy." There was genuine concern in her voice.

I didn't like the sound of what Molly had said. Following her into the puppy house, I picked up a few of the lethargic puppies and examined them. At seven weeks old, puppies are known for their excessive and boundless energy. This bunch seemed anything but that. I had a bad feeling we were facing a parvo outbreak.

Canine parvovirus type 2, or parvo as it's more commonly called, is a highly contagious and often fatal disease that invades the gastrointestinal tract of puppies and dogs. Usually less than half of puppies afflicted with parvo survive. Although a series of vaccines can prevent parvo, it most often threatens the health of puppies that haven't yet received all their shots. What's worse is that most deaths from parvo happen within forty-eight to seventy-two hours after the first clinical signs.

I immediately called our veterinarian and shared what I suspected. He told me to bring in several of the pups for an examination right away. Molly and Alix accompanied me as we transported the sickest of the group.

Unfortunately, Doc confirmed my suspicion and explained that we basically had two choices. "Because parvovirus is a virus, there's not much we can do to treat it," he said. "Sadly, most of the puppies probably won't survive, so you could put them to sleep now and eliminate any suffering on their end. The other choice is to offer what we call supportive care and hope for the best."

"What does supportive care mean?" Alix asked.

"It means that we put all of the sick puppies in the hospital, we give them medicine to control their vomiting and diarrhea, and we try to prevent dehydration. It can be very expensive, and the outcome isn't always successful. When a dog has parvo, time is of the essence, so we would need to start treatment immediately."

I quickly did the math in my head. Hospitalization was out of the question.

"With twenty-one puppies possibly afflicted, we

obviously can't afford to hospitalize all of them," I said. "Is there anything else that can be done?"

Luckily for us, Doc had been a strong ally from the beginning. Staying true to form, he quickly offered another option.

"Well, I can teach you how to administer subcutaneous fluids and you can monitor the pups back at the shelter instead of hospitalizing them here. It won't be easy and it will require a lot of extra work since you'll have to treat all the puppies with medicine twice a day, plus give them fluids to keep them hydrated."

I took a deep breath and tried to calm my racing mind. I needed only to look at Alix's and Molly's pleading faces to know what our decision had to be.

"Okay," I said. "I think we have our answer. Let's do this!"

As we headed back to the shelter, I called Katie to give her a heads-up about our impromptu plan. She shared our love of animals and was spending her summer home from college helping Mark and me. But after seeing how much work was involved in running the sanctuary, she had already decided she would not return to college in the fall, but instead, devote all her time to working at the shelter. From fundraising to giving puppy vaccinations, Katie became our "jill-of-all-trades." But her greatest contribution was serving as a role model for my students, especially the young girls. I knew if we had any chance of saving these parvo puppies, Katie would have to play a key role.

Later that afternoon, Doc came out to the shelter, bringing all the drugs and supplies we needed to treat the sick puppies. He examined each of our patients and determined the proper amount of medicine and fluids for each one. The kids created a chart, which we taped to the wall so we could keep track of the medications, the feedings, and the responses from each puppy.

Doc then showed Katie and me how to give the puppies their medicine. Subcutaneous therapy is the fastest way to get fluids and medications into the body, and since the puppies were so sick, we needed to act quickly. And although I felt confident after Doc's one-on-one training, my heart still sank as he got into his truck and drove away.

It was up to us now to help the puppies survive over the next several days. Their fate rested solely in our hands.

Katie and I started medicating the rest of the puppies. Although we were approaching the evening hours, the air still carried the day's heat. A few small beads of perspiration trickled down my back. I wasn't sure if the sweat was due to the excessive temperatures or my rising anxiety.

"Mrs. Trull, can we stay and help you?" Alix asked, a pleading look in her eyes. "All of our afternoon chores are done, but we're not ready to leave yet. Maybe we can hold the puppies after you've given them their medicine?"

Alix had a strong affinity for animals of all kinds and would find any excuse to be around them. The unspoken beauty of DAWGS was that it served a dual purpose: not only was it a haven for countless animals, but it was also a sanctuary for many of the children who spent time there, including Alix.

"I don't see why not," I replied. Secretly, I welcomed the idea of having the kids around to love on the puppies.

As hard as it may be to believe, we still didn't have any electricity at the shelter, even though we had already been open for months, and we were struggling to operate with the limited water supply on site. Mark was constantly battling with the city officials about the time frame for getting our utilities hooked up. Their answer was always an elusive "We're working on it." The lack of basic services made the simplest of chores more challenging.

Since the days had grown long with the summer, we had the luxury of completing our outdoor rounds under the waning daylight. But because all our puppies were living inside one of the buildings, we desperately needed light to see what we were doing. The seventy-year-old house, which we had lovingly nicknamed "the nursery," had two small wooden doors with high archways gracing the exterior, but it had no windows. The shadows inside the building made it almost impossible to see.

Before Doc showed up, we'd transformed the interior into a makeshift hospital ward. The kids had already rigorously cleaned and disinfected the space. Wires were strung across the room with clear bags of fluid hanging down. Twenty-one strands of IV tubing waved like streamers on a spring maypole. Fuzzy towels kept our patients warm.

Mark stopped by the shelter to see if we needed any help treating the puppies. When he saw our predicament with the lack of light, he suggested we open the doors, pull our trucks up as close as we could, and turn on the high beams. His creative suggestion was the perfect solution.

Over the next few hours, Katie and I gingerly treated each puppy with medicine and fluids. Some of the puppies were so tiny and frail. In between each of the treatments, six of our young volunteers lovingly cradled the sick puppies and offered sweet prayers for each one. We tried to prepare the children that all the puppies might not make it. In spite of our sobering conversations, a calmness and serenity penetrated the building.

Four times a day, we repeated the gentle ministering. And night after night, each puppy was loved on and prayed over for a healthy recovery.

By the end of the week, we were through the worst of the crisis. Amazingly, we lost only three puppies from the twenty-one that were sick. But even losing three lives had a profound effect on the children.

"It's so sad that all the puppies didn't make it," Molly confided to Mark and me after the third puppy had passed away. She was helping us move fifty-pound bags of dry dog food from several wooden pallets into the metal storage shed. Her face glistened with sweat from the midday heat.

"Well, we certainly did everything we could to save them," Mark assured her. "I know it hurts when we lose an animal. We just need to do our best and understand that Mother Nature usually knows what she's doing."

"I know, but they were all so cute," Molly lamented. "I really wish we could have saved all of the puppies. I guess it's all God's plan."

"It's okay to feel sad sometimes, Molly," Mark said, pausing to wipe his brow with a towel. "You want to be a person who shows compassion toward others, be it people or animals. It's not a good idea to stuff your emotions away just because they're painful or because you're afraid of what others might say about you. Mourning those we've lost is a healthy reaction. But don't lose sight of the fact that, because of everybody's hard work, a lot of lives were saved."

After a few minutes of companionable silence,

Molly said, "You know what I think we should do? I think we should find a special place where we can bury the pups and have a funeral."

"I think that's a fine idea, Molly," I said.

As soon as all the food was neatly stacked in the shed, Molly recruited a few of her fellow volunteers. She told them about her idea, and they chose a special area on the west side of the property to bury the deceased. For several hours, the kids painstakingly collected an assortment of rocks, stones, and pebbles and laid them out in the shape of a large heart on the ground. They christened the area "The Little Angels Cemetery."

The next afternoon, we held an informal funeral service. Mark had dug a hole large enough so we could properly bury the three puppies. Everybody in the group held hands and said a few prayers for the ones that didn't make it.

When the ceremony was over, the kids wiped the tears from their eyes, straightened their slim little shoulders, then picked up their plastic food buckets and went back to feeding the rest of the dogs. While it was important for them to honor the dead, they were eager to get back to the tremendous task of caring for the hundreds of animals that were so dependent on them.

In its purest form, I knew I had just witnessed a heartrending moment balanced by heartwarming determination.

CHAPTER 6
Soul Work

■ ■ ■ ■ ■

RORY

Rory was an adorable mix who had a rough start in life. Rory's homeless mother had been found during a terrible blizzard and within a few days gave birth to four little ones. The dedicated mom took great care of her babies, but they were all very frail due to her having been on the street for so long. Sadly, at eight weeks old, all the puppies became sick with parvo and were in and out of the veterinarian's office for a month.

When they were well enough to go on our mobile adoptions, sweet Rory was quickly adopted. Six months later, Rory's adopter brought him back to us because he was moving and couldn't take the dog with him.

Rory was so adorable. He would play bow to everyone, especially small children. Some of my students taught him how to shake hands. Rory loved to lay on people's feet and would often take his kibble and share it with anybody he met.

We began taking Rory to our adoption events again. When a little girl saw Rory, she exclaimed to her mom, "Want woowoo!", which apparently means dog in child speak, and Rory was adopted into his forever family.

■ ■ ■ ■ ■

SCHOOL HAD STARTED AGAIN and I had a new group of fourth graders. On most days, it didn't take long for my car to fill up with students wanting a ride to the shelter after the last bell had rung. Truth be told, I probably could have loaded up a Greyhound bus with the number of kids who were eager to help. To say they were anxious to be with the dogs would be an understatement.

The number of children who volunteered grew as the shelter grew. About one hundred and twenty students—almost half of our school's student body—participated in some form or fashion. Not all the kids showed up every day. A handful came every few weeks. Some brought their siblings. Others brought their friends who attended different schools. But regardless of who was volunteering, every student had to abide by our five basic rules:

1. Everybody must have their parents' permission before they could start volunteering.
2. All homework and home chores must be done.
3. Good grades must always be maintained while working at the shelter.
4. Sunday mornings are reserved for families and church.
5. Everybody must have outside interests beyond working at the sanctuary.

As grateful as we were for the children's dedication to helping care for the animals, the last requirement about having other interests was something Mark and I strongly believed in and constantly encouraged. For us to be successful at the shelter, we had to be sure that our kids prioritized what was important in their lives and learned how to balance their activities. Then, if they had any time left on their calendars, we encouraged them to come out and spend it with us.

As a result, the students' level of involvement fluctuated with other events in their lives. It wasn't that their commitment to helping at the sanctuary tapered off; the reality was, they just had fewer hours to volunteer as they got more involved in extracurricular activities. The boys played football, basketball, baseball, and ran track. Many of the girls played on the school's basketball, volleyball, and softball teams. Others were cheerleaders. Depending on which sports season was underway, we didn't see the students as much at the shelter. But when those sports were over, everybody quickly reappeared in full force.

Despite our rules, there were still times when Mark and I had to intervene if we felt that any student was spending too much time at the shelter. Such was the case with Lauren. Lauren and her brother Zachary, who was one of my students, found refuge spending time at the shelter. Lauren was fourteen years old when she started volunteering. She quickly settled in as a competent and dedicated worker. So much so that her grades began to suffer.

"Lauren, I hate to be the bearer of bad news, but Mrs. Trull and I have decided that you need to stay home for a few days," Mark said, breaking the news to her as gently as he could when she showed up at the shelter one Saturday.

"But why?" Lauren replied, obviously crestfallen. "Has something happened?"

"We've learned your grades are starting to slip, and we just can't let that happen," Mark explained. "We all feel that you are spending too much time out here, after school and on the weekends."

"But it makes me feel so happy being with all the dogs."

"I understand," Mark said. "But without good grades, you'll have a hard time doing something positive with your life after high school. So, let's focus on getting your grades up again and then we'll figure out a new schedule that gives you enough time to study as well as volunteer. And I promise there will still be plenty of Snickers waiting for you when you return."

Because Mark knew that Lauren had a sweet tooth, he would often hide Snickers candy bars around the shelter for her to find. He had a soft spot for all the children and would find ways of making them feel special.

"SO, WHO'S GOING to work together this afternoon?" I asked the kids who had hopped into my car. It was a question I asked the volunteers every day because the number of animals in our care had quickly spiked to more than one hundred and fifty. With so many animals, being organized was critical to our operation. Mark and I encouraged the kids to pair up with different classmates so they could learn the value of cooperation and teamwork. It also taught them that if somebody wasn't doing their job, they were messing it up for everybody else, especially the dogs.

"Yesterday, Kelsey and I fed the adult dogs," Molly said. "Today, I'd really like to be inside with all the puppies."

"I'll help you," Alix said eagerly. She rarely passed up an opportunity to be on puppy detail. Her nurturing skills were at their best when there were young dogs in need of extra care and attention.

"Chipper is my favorite one right now," Molly continued.

He was one of four border collie puppies born in our shelter a few months prior.

"He's so cute," she said. "He lets me hold him and pet him and take him on walks. He's the kind of dog I would love to have some day."

Molly's family owned a working dog, canines that are bred to have certain physical and mental abilities to assist their owners in performing certain jobs. Although they can be wonderful companions, most working dogs don't become official family pets until they are too old to perform their working dog responsibilities. Owning a working dog only underscored the reason why Molly was so keen to have a dog of her own.

Whenever I reminded her to be patient about getting a family pet, her response was often, "I guess I'll have to put it in God's hands then."

"Well, no matter how many dogs there are, we just have to be careful that we don't skip anybody because they're all important," Alix said. "They all have feelings too."

"I think Miss Cindy came in earlier this afternoon to start feeding the puppies," I said. "We'll have to check with her first to see how far she got."

Cindy was one of our most regular and dedicated adult volunteers. She and her family had moved to Dalhart from Colorado, where she had been actively involved with several animal rescue groups. We had only been in operation for a few weeks when she came to see me about volunteer opportunities. She was shocked to learn there wasn't already a waiting list of volunteers. Apparently, the shelters in Colorado were blessed with an overabundance of people anxious to donate their time.

"Unfortunately, we don't have that same problem here," I remember telling her. "I'm thrilled that you want to help. We always need extra hands and you can begin as soon as you like."

"Let me start with coming out on the weekends," Cindy said. "We'll see how things go from there."

It didn't take long for Cindy to become a permanent fixture at the sanctuary, working ten to eleven hours nearly every weekday. She would also cover for us on the weekends when Mark and I traveled to Amarillo to hold our weekly pet adoptions.

Cindy loved mentoring the kids and patiently taught them the proper way to care for the animals. She also firmly believed that the dogs learned from our interactions and contact with them. She had a standing rule for all volunteers and workers, regardless of age, that nobody entered a pen to feed, clean, or set up a water bucket without taking the time to recognize the dogs in the pen, to love them, and talk to them. She constantly reminded us that we were the only human contact the dogs currently had, so it was up to us to make sure that each encounter was a positive one.

Surprisingly, many shelters don't encourage children's involvement, for fear of liability. As a result, most children don't understand the depth of the animal homelessness problem in this country or what it takes to solve it. But listening to my students' enthusiasm about their work, I can't help but feel that other groups are missing out on a great opportunity to help mold wonderful citizens. We choose to actively promote the involvement of children in our work because they are our future. In particular, children between the ages of six and eleven have the greatest capacity for compassion and it's a shame we close that door on them. They are the ones who are going to make a difference. Personally, I would like each one of them to have as much compassion for animals as possible.

"So, I'm curious about something," I said to the students as we bumped along the dirt road. "It's obvious how your volunteering helps the dogs. But have you ever thought about how it's helping you personally, especially when you could be doing something more fun instead of giving up all of your free time to be at the shelter?"

"Although it sometimes feels like a job, I love dogs and I want them to have lives just like we do," Molly said. "And coming to work at the shelter every day is definitely helping me with my homework. I have to be better organized now since I'm spending so much time up here. My parents keep telling me that I have to keep up my grades at school, no matter what."

"And your parents are right," I said. "Getting good grades in school is so important in helping you get into college or finding a good job after high school. The better your grades, the more academic and career choices you will have."

Molly added, "And I think spending all this time with the animals has made me realize I might want to be a veterinarian when I grow up."

I wasn't totally surprised by Molly's announcement. With the kids' constant exposure to so many animals in need, I assumed somebody in the group would express an interest in becoming a veterinarian.

"Well, you'll definitely need good grades if you want to get into veterinary school," I said. "It's a lot of work, but it can be a very rewarding job.

"So, back to my original question. Jesse, what do you think volunteering has changed in your life?"

Jesse was wearing his thinking face and hesitated a few minutes before answering. "I guess I'm not as lazy as I used to be," he finally shared. "I like playing video games and watching television as much as anybody else, but now that I know there are a bunch of dogs out here depending on me for food and water and going for walks, I don't have time for that stuff anymore. The pens need to be cleaned and the dogs need to be played with. It's up to us to come out here every day after school and get the work done."

"Do you miss playing your video games?" I asked.

"Nah, not really. You know, it's really hard for me not to be thinking about the dogs all the time now and how we can make their lives better. Being at the shelter is definitely the best part of my day!"

"And Alix, what about you?" I asked, glancing at her in my rearview mirror.

"Well, it's made me realize how important it is to keep a commitment once you make it," she said. "We all said we wanted to help the animals, so we can't just quit because we're tired or something. No matter if it's raining or snowing, the dogs need us. It's like these dogs are our pets. I want to do my part to make sure that each one of our dogs gets to have a wonderful life. And it makes me feel so happy just being with them."

"I'm glad to hear that all of you can see what a difference volunteering is making in your lives," I said. "It's a good feeling to be able to give back to the animals and to the community, but it's also important to understand how it's positively impacting your life."

"Mrs. Trull, do you know what the hardest thing is about volunteering at the shelter?" Jesse asked.

"No." I waited.

"Well, believe it or not, it's when a dog gets adopted," he said. "I mean, it makes me feel really happy because they're finally getting a new home, but it's like letting go of one of my very own pets."

"I know," I assured Jesse. "I feel the same way, but we can't keep all of them. And when a dog gets adopted that means we have more room to take in another dog that needs a second chance. That's why we do what we do."

And I did understand Jesse's mixed emotions. It is very bittersweet when our dogs move out. Some of them come to us seriously ill or depressed and we spend a lot of time and energy nurturing them back to health. We love and care for them as we would our own pets. We celebrate the fact that we have saved so many animals and rejoice each time they walk out of the shelter and into the arms of a loving family.

But, inevitably, the children get more attached to certain animals, and when their favorite ones leave, they cry. We started calling those moments "tears of happiness." We are so happy when the dogs find a home, but so sad to see them go. At the end of the day, the kids know they have played an important role in helping that dog get adopted. And that feeling of doing something good helps them to feel better about themselves.

"So, I've got a surprise for you," I continued. "One of the local television stations called me a few days ago to request an interview for a feature they want to run about the sanctuary in an upcoming newscast. The reporter, Maeghan, stated that she wanted to focus the story on how we rehabilitate the dogs and get them ready for adoption.

"The reporter and her cameraman are coming to the sanctuary later this afternoon. I've encouraged her to interview as many of you as possible since you're the ones responsible for finding the right companions for the dogs and offering them plenty of playtime and socialization."

"Wow, that's pretty cool," Alix said. "Are we really going to be on TV?"

"Well, only if you want to be," I said. "But I think it's important for everybody in Dalhart to see how hard you all are working and that you're the reason for the shelter's success. Plus, it might encourage other kids to get involved in something they believe in."

"Wait until the kids at school find out about this!" Jesse exclaimed.

When the reporter arrived, I offered to give her a brief tour of our facilities. As we walked around the property, I explained to her that no animal can be adopted without being spayed or neutered and microchipped.

"Texas state law requires that any animal adopted from a shelter must be sterilized," I said. "Failure to comply is a criminal offense categorized as a Class C misdemeanor. The result is a minimum five-hundred-dollar fine and repossession of the animal. If an animal is too young for surgery at the time of adoption, a substantial deposit is required that is then refunded when the owner shows proof that the animal has been fixed.

"Unfortunately, this law doesn't stop people

from dropping off their unwanted puppies here at the sanctuary. But when that happens, we try to convince the owners to do the right thing and get the parent dogs fixed so we can stop the heartbreaking cycle of unwanted births."

I also explained about our return policy, which each prospective owner must agree to as part of our adoption agreement. The addendum pays tribute to Nano, a sweet husky mix; he was tragically put to sleep when his owner couldn't deal with him.

"Nano was adopted by a young woman and her friend," I said. "Our policy is to call each owner within a few days after adoption to see how everybody is getting along. When we called Nano's owner, the woman mentioned that Nano was having some anxiety issues, but she wanted to work through them. A few days later, she left us a voicemail requesting that Nano be picked up because the situation had worsened. After several unsuccessful attempts to contact the owner to coordinate a pickup time, we left her a message saying that we would be at her house by six o'clock that evening to pick up Nano. Before we left, however, we got a phone call from Amarillo Animal Control telling us that the woman had called them before calling us and requested that the dog be put down immediately. We were all heartbroken.

"The addendum states that if an adoption

doesn't work out for any reason, the owners must contact DAWGS and allow us ample time to retrieve the adopted animal. Failure to do so will result in a five-hundred-dollar fine. We created this addendum so there won't be any more dogs like Nano that suffer such a horrible end. We realize the fine isn't enforceable, but when people are debating between contacting us versus abandoning the dog or killing it, it can be a strong motivator to do what is right for the animal.

"Okay, I think I've talked long enough about all the legal stuff. Now you should visit with some of the kids and learn firsthand about what life is really like at the sanctuary."

We found a group of young volunteers cleaning out some of the dog runs toward the front of the shelter. As we approached, we could hear their laughter as they sprayed each other with water from the garden hose.

"During the warmer months and rainstorms, this is why the kids' attire turns into shorts and tall rubber boots!" I said, smiling at their playfulness.

Once the kids had dried off, they were anxious to share their thoughts and experiences with the reporter. I stood off to the side listening to the interview.

The reporter first asked them to explain the dogs' living arrangements.

"We are really careful about which dogs we put

together in each of the kennels," Jesse explained with a serious look. "It's important to make sure they get along well with each other. Some of them had a hard life out on their own, so they need extra time to feel safe again. It's important which dogs they get paired with because it can really make a difference in helping them feel good about themselves and eventually find a perfect home."

I marveled at Jesse's little speech. Even though he had always thought with an adult perspective, it wasn't too long ago that he would have been reluctant to share his thoughts or opinions, especially with strangers around. My heart swelled as I watched how confident he appeared in front of the television camera.

"It's good to work out here because the dogs don't die in a couple of days," Lauren said. "I disagree with anyone who thinks they should die. They deserve a life too, a good one. And we try everything we can to make sure that happens. They're not just dogs; they have human characteristics, too. They have feelings. They have hearts that beat. They're lovable and nurturing just like people can be."

"I feel the same way," Molly added. "And whenever we get a new dog, we take it to the veterinarian right away so it can be examined and get all of its shots. If we get a bunch of dogs in at the same time, we sometimes have to make eight to ten trips to the vet every week. And that doesn't include making appointments for them to be spayed or neutered. We do everything we can to save as many of them as possible."

"We took an action to help animals and not just sit around and watch television all day," Alix continued. "We wanted to come out here and help. Through no fault of their own, many of the animals we rescue have been hurt, abused, or abandoned. We're here because we want to be here. I feel like all of these dogs are mine and I have to be responsible so I can take care of these babies."

When the interview with the kids was over, I urged the reporter to also interview Mark since he is such an important member of our team. He had recently taken a six-month leave of absence from his job as a corporate recruiter to help work at the sanctuary full-time. I couldn't do half of what I do if it wasn't for all of his help and support, emotionally and physically.

We found him fixing some fence posts at the back of the property. The sanctuary always has something in need of repair, and Mark is usually the one providing the manual labor. He seemed happy to have a reason to take a break.

"Tell me about the philosophy of what you're trying to accomplish with this shelter," the reporter asked him.

"One of the primary tenets of DAWGS is that

we don't just take in the easy-to-adopt dogs," Mark said. "Diane and I insist on teaching that compassion shouldn't be saved for only the young and the beautiful. This whole process is about setting an example for the kids.

"Except for a handful of vicious dogs and a few that were either too ill to be saved or terminally injured, we have taken in every dog that has gone unclaimed at the city pound—mixed-breed and purebred, young and old, homely and lame, sick and injured. And, because of our policy, the city pound has been uncharacteristically empty at times, sometimes for as long as a week straight.

"Beyond caring for the animals, though, we're also trying to teach the kids that some things are really important in life, and they're not necessarily the things that other people see you do. We talk about integrity and responsibility and owning your actions. When they come to the shelter, the kids get immediate reinforcement of that behavior because they see the benefit of feeding and watering a dog and developing a bond with the animal they're taking care of. When the gate shuts at night, they know the dogs can't take care of themselves.

"I worry that we're raising a generation of kids who think someone else will take care of all the problems. I think you have to give back to the community. It's pretty hypocritical to have parents or leaders sitting on their couches with television remotes in their hands, preaching to their kids about commitment and sacrifice."

When the interview was over, I walked the reporter and the cameraman back to the front gate and thanked them for their interest in what we were trying to accomplish. Both commented on how impressed they were with the children's dedication and work ethic.

"That's the key to what makes this work as well as it does," I said. "There are many adults who want to make a difference in something they believe in, but they don't see how their individual contribution will matter, so they end up doing nothing. Feeling powerless can lead to frustration and hopelessness, which often results in inaction. But these kids don't necessarily look at the end result. Instead, they show up every day, no matter how bad the weather is and do their small part, and the difference happens gradually over time because of their collective effort. It's another great example of how children can teach adults valuable life lessons."

CHAPTER 7

Staking a Claim

■ ■ ■ ■ ■

COPPER

One of the most critically injured dogs we ever received was Copper, a young bloodhound. Copper had been hit by a truck outside the city of Amarillo. A deliveryman saw the accident in his rearview mirror and watched as the truck that hit the animal pulled over. The delivery-man assumed the big dog would be okay and continued on his journey.

Two days later, the man's delivery route required him to go back through the same area where he had traveled a few days prior. He was shocked to see the bloodhound still lying on the side of the road. The man quickly stopped and found Copper was still alive, but he was very dehydrated and had several injuries. The man brought the dog to us and we took him to a local veterinarian where he was diagnosed with leg injuries and a broken pelvis. Copper quickly mended except for the pelvis injury, which required him to be confined for one hundred days.

A young bloodhound confined to a small space is NOT a happy dog! Copper howled nonstop so he had an assigned helper for the entire time we were at the shelter. He seemed less anxious and relieved to have a buddy to pet him and love on him. Although a little wobbly, Copper was finally able to start going for walks. He was so happy to be out and about.

With the help of a great bloodhound rescue group in Colorado, we transported Copper to his forever home where he enjoys being pampered and loved.

■ ■ ■ ■ ■

SINCE OPENING THE DALHART Animal Wellness Group and Sanctuary six months ago, we have accepted almost three hundred dogs into our program," I reported at the September city council meeting. "We are proud to report that one hundred and twenty-five of these dogs have been adopted. However, we are currently at capacity, housing one hundred and forty-nine animals."

At the start of the meeting, the mayor acknowledged that tonight was Dalhart's most-attended city council meeting in history. Many groups were well represented in the audience, including area residents, the local media, and employees from the school. The reason for the extraordinary turnout was item number four on the council's agenda: Update on Animal Shelter. I was baffled as to why our efforts to help homeless animals was garnering such interest.

Going into this meeting, my intention was to outline several projects and improvements that Mark and I felt were absolutely necessary to get us through the winter. The frigid days pass slowly in Dalhart, and I wanted to be prepared for the long, chilly season ahead. Our hope was to lobby for the council's support in the form of some much-needed funding. Instead, the meeting turned into a passionate, somewhat strained debate about what we were doing. The question of "numbers" surfaced again and again.

"When you first started this thing, there were twenty-five dogs," the mayor said. "Just how big is it going to get?"

"We would love to see the numbers drop back to twenty-five," Mark responded. "Truthfully, we'd love to see it at zero, but that's not something we can control. Until people see the importance and the necessity of spaying and neutering their pets, our numbers are not going to decrease. What we need from the city council and you, Mayor, is to know that you are behind this program. We need to know that we have everybody's support."

"If I may interrupt, please." A man in the audience raised his hand. It was the pastor of Lakeview United Methodist Church. "Instead of focusing on numbers and statistics, I would like to praise the group for what they are accomplishing. I often take members from our youth group to the shelter to help walk the dogs. It's a great environment where children learn important virtues, such as responsibility and compassion. The kids are devoted to this cause, and Mark and Diane are serving as important role models for many of these children. We are lucky to have this sanctuary in our hometown and we should be proud of what is being accomplished out there every single day. I personally support and applaud their efforts."

"I think it's also worth noting," added the Dalhart police chief, "that because of the sanctuary, there is a wonderful difference in the number of stray dogs running loose on our town's streets. We're not seeing as many dogs as we used to."

"Diane and Mark, we certainly applaud the

achievements of what you and all the children have done in a short period of time," one of the councilmen said. "The city will do what it can to help the organization, but we are also fiscally responsible for the entire city."

"It has never been our intention for the city to support our facility indefinitely," I said, struggling to keep my voice level. "All we're asking for is a little help in getting through the next few months. There are various organizations and individuals from all over the country helping us with some of our current expenses. We've also applied for grant money from several foundations, but there is a waiting period while they verify that we're a credible operation. By spring, we should be eligible to start receiving some of those funds. And, there is also some expected revenue coming from the schools participating in our recycling program, which is not in full swing yet."

"Okay, I think the next step is for you to prioritize the projects that you have in mind and we'll review them," the mayor suggested. "I'd like to request that a few of the council members form a subcommittee to study the shelter's requests, prioritize the items that we will consider helping with, and bring the list to the next council meeting."

Two days later I submitted a detailed report, which Mark and I had carefully prepared, outlining the shelter's needs for the next six months. I crossed my fingers when I dropped off the document at the council chambers.

The following month, we found ourselves back at city hall for the October city council meeting. And to my continued amazement, there was once again a significant number of residents in attendance.

"There's a misconception out there that the shelter has to be funded on an ongoing basis by the city, but that is simply not true," Mark said in his opening remarks to the council members. "It's not fair for the taxpayers of this community to put money into something that they don't see an immediate benefit for."

Mark and I were prepared to lobby hard for what we needed.

He continued. "We understand that the council has to be extremely judicious in how it looks at projects in the community and what it feels it needs to support. But there are a lot of things that support a community that initially do not have obvious benefits. In other communities that have established spay-and-neuter programs, it takes about three to four years to see the results of taking stray dogs off the street.

"When we first talked about starting this shelter, we were thinking it would be fifteen or twenty dogs maximum. It's long past that now. More than one hundred and thirty dogs have been adopted since our program began, and we currently have close to one hundred and sixty dogs in our care. Diane and I are constantly looking for ways to support this project. Politically and financially, it can't fall on the city's shoulders. We know that. But like any project that gets started with an underestimation of its implications, there are times when assistance is needed to make sure that it doesn't fall off and hit the side of the cliff."

"We believe this project isn't just about the animals either," I interjected. "As a community, do we want to support a project where kids are willing to give up their free time that's usually spent watching television or playing video games? There are a handful of students at the shelter every day helping as many dogs as they can. And they're not just doing the fun stuff. They're shoveling dog poop, walking through mud and muck, carrying fifty-pound bags of dog food, and filling up water bowls. They're learning responsibility and then taking that sense of responsibility home and sharing it with their family. Many of the kids have settled in as competent, caring, and dedicated workers.

"It makes sense to have our kids involved in doing something that's beneficial to the community. It makes sense to teach them responsibility. It makes sense to take stray animals off the street and not kill six hundred dogs a year. If the community believes in these assumptions, then I think there should be a partnership in which the community looks to us to help solve this problem. We can't solve all the problems with the sanctuary, but it's a step."

Although my voice was shaky, I continued with my plea. "We have people sending donations from all over the United States right now. They have heard about what we're doing, and they want to know how a bunch of school kids can achieve this. This is a shining star for Dalhart."

Mark jumped in. "Even if you come back tonight and say 'we have nothing to give you,' DAWGS is going to survive. Are we going to have some dogs that are uncomfortable? No doubt. Are we going to have some dogs that are going to be very cold? You bet. But the issue on the table is determining if this project is important enough for the community to support. Five to ten years from now, what do we want our community to look like?"

"Your comments are pretty close to right," the mayor said. "We started this with the idea that it would be a no-kill facility. It has certainly snowballed. We had no idea it would go this far. I guess nobody did. Council members, are you prepared to report on the findings of the subcommittee assigned to consider the funding that the shelter has requested?"

"We are," one of the council members said, straightening some papers in front of her. "There are a few things that we feel the city should take responsibility for fixing. Although we didn't come up with an exact dollar amount, we agree that the city should help the shelter with installing the water lines. However, the subcommittee is reluctant to release all the money currently in reserve to cover these expenses."

The mayor pointed out that the city would continue to take the responsibility of rounding up the stray dogs, feeding them, and holding them for three days before turning them over to DAWGS. They would also continue to euthanize the ones that were vicious or very sick.

"Hopefully, we can hold hands and go with this thing as long as we can," one of the councilmen said. "And we're very grateful that you realize we don't have all kinds of money to throw at your operation at this time. What we can give you are 'atta boys' and pats on the back, and hope for the best."

The mayor introduced a motion in which the city would provide minimum assistance to help our facility get through the Panhandle's notorious harsh winter. "The ultimate goal is that we can sit back and be proud of you," he said.

The council approved the motion and agreed to release two thousand dollars to correct the water and plumbing problems. "This amount still leaves some money in the animal control budget for emergencies," the mayor said. "It's the best we can do without making any budget amendments. And that would be difficult to do since we haven't done that for any other group."

We thanked the council members for their support and left the meeting feeling a little more hopeful than when we had walked in. Thanks to a grant we had recently secured from the local utility company, we finally had electricity at the shelter. And with the promise of unlimited water soon to come, things were definitely looking up.

CHAPTER 8
Big City Lights

■ ■ ■ ■ ■

Photo by Diane Trull

SWEETPEA

Sweetpea was a darling miniature pinscher that was found in a deserted house hiding among some garbage and discarded waste. The dog had been left alone for more than two weeks without food or water. In addition to being very hungry and scared, she was also very pregnant and tried to bite anyone who came near her.

We managed to get close enough and carefully wrapped all six pounds of her in a blanket and took her straight to the veterinarian. The doctor was concerned about her vision and general poor health but released her with some medicine. During the night, Sweetpea gave birth to four stillborn puppies. She then became extremely ill. Within a few days, she was doing better, but had developed severe eye issues, causing her to be temporarily blind. We nursed her through two months of antibiotics and vitamins, and gradually her vision came back.

One day, a nice couple came to the shelter looking to adopt a small dog, having lost their previous pet to cancer a few months before. They fell in love with Sweetpea and took her home. When we did a follow-up visit to see how things were going, we found Sweetpea curled up in a big recliner chair, watching a football game with her new family.

■ ■ ■ ■ ■

I THOUGHT IT HAD TO BE a prank call when the woman on the other end of the phone identified herself as Natasha Allas, Miss World USA 2000. Why on earth would somebody with that much prestige be contacting me?

"I'm calling on behalf of an organization called In Defense of Animals," Natasha explained. "IDA is an international animal rights and rescue group based in California. They are dedicated to protecting the rights, welfare, and habitats of animals. Before you start thinking that this is a sales call asking for a donation, I promise you it's not. Instead, I'm calling to share some exciting news that involves IDA and your shelter.

"This year, 2003, marks the twentieth anniversary of the nonprofit group. To celebrate this milestone, IDA is hosting a gala in October where they will present special awards to those individuals or groups, who act as guardians of animals rather than as owners. Renowned primatologist Dr. Jane Goodall is going to be the guest of honor at the event. IDA will present her with a Lifetime Achievement Award for her long-term study of wild chimpanzees in Tanzania. In addition, several deserving organizations will receive Guardian Awards for their tireless efforts in animal rescue.

"When IDA learned about the efforts of your students, they wanted to honor their accomplishments too, so they established a Distinguished Youth Guardian Award. I'm happy to tell you that DAWGS will be the first recipient of this very special recognition."

I hesitated a moment to give myself time to think of a response. "I really don't know what to say," I said. "To be recognized by such a prominent group is very humbling. And to be mentioned in the same circle as Dr. Goodall is almost surreal. My kids work so hard trying to make a difference for all the animals in our care.

I know how excited they will be when they learn about this award."

"Well, there's more to it than just an award," Natasha said. "IDA would like to invite you and one of your students—the one who best represents the class—on an all-expenses-paid trip next month to attend the First Annual Guardian Awards Gala in Santa Monica, California, to receive the award in person. It's a black-tie affair that will be hosted by actors John O'Hurley and Pierce Brosnan. It should be quite a star-studded evening!"

"Oh, how exciting!" I exclaimed. "We would be honored to attend. Thank you so much. I will have to get back to you, though, on which child will be attending. All of them work so hard in caring for the animals, it will be hard to pick just one. Plus, most of my students have never been outside of Dalhart before, let alone been on an airplane, so this will be a big deal for them."

After I hung up, my mind started racing—how would we decide which student got to go? They were all so deserving, and I didn't want any of them to feel less special or left out. I was touched by the news of the call and recognized that this was a good problem to be facing. The students were constantly facing negativism from people in the community and here was a chance for them to realize what they were doing was so special.

However, my happy little bubble quickly burst

when Cindy called me a few minutes later on my cell.

"Diane, I wanted to get a jump start on feeding the animals, but it doesn't look like there's enough food in the storage shed to feed everybody," she said. "What do you want me to do?"

The financial health of our shelter rose and fell depending on our intake numbers. We had taken in quite a few animals recently so I knew our funds were low. What I didn't realize was that our food supply was also low.

"We received a shipment of dog food yesterday from one of the major pet food companies," I said. "They're introducing a new line of food and sent us some to try. Unfortunately, what they sent were hundreds of small sample bags. I don't know what else to do at this point but to ask if you would mind opening up all those little packages."

"Well, if that's all that we have right now, then I guess I better get busy," she said. And once again, I marveled at her willingness to do whatever it takes to help the animals.

I don't know how many hours it took Cindy to open all the packets, but by the time the kids and I arrived after school, there were several wheelbarrows full of food so they could start feeding the dogs immediately. Cindy's labor of love made it possible for us to scrape through another day.

Later that night when Mark and I were finally home together, I told him about the invitation to the gala and the dilemma of only being able to bring one student. We felt that it would be great if several students could attend and decided to hold a couple of fundraisers in the hope of raising money to cover the cost of sending a few more kids to California.

A few weeks later, I called Natasha back and gave her an update. She laughed when I told her there would be a small army of us coming to the event instead of just the two representatives.

"I couldn't bear the thought of having to choose only one of my students to attend the gala; they're all so deserving," I explained to her. "We held a couple of bake sales and had a lemonade stand and raised enough money to cover the expenses for five more of us to fly out. This just goes to show how determined my kids are when they put their minds to something. I hope that's not going to cause a problem."

Natasha was extremely gracious and assured me that having additional students in attendance would only make the evening more special.

THE MORNING OF the gala, four of my students—Kali, Kelsey, Molly, and Ally—plus Kelsey's mom, Sandy, Katie, and I boarded a plane bright and early and headed to California.

It was a whirlwind trip from the moment we

landed. One of the first things the girls wanted to do was visit Grauman's Chinese Theatre and its hundreds of handprints, footprints, and autographs of Hollywood celebrities on display. We were wearing special T-shirts that one of my student's mother made for our trip. Because the shirts were a bright blue, it was easy to spot us in a crowd.

We were on the Hollywood Walk of Fame when we were stopped by a man carrying a large folder. "Excuse me, can I talk to you for a minute?"

"Sure," I said, although I was a bit skeptical about what he wanted.

"What does DAWGS stand for?" he asked, pointing to our matching shirts.

"These are my fourth-grade students and we run an animal rescue shelter in Texas," I said. "DAWGS stands for Dalhart Animal Wellness Group and Sanctuary. We're here because we're being honored at a gala this evening."

"Wow, that's really great," the man said. "Would you have time to come to the taping of *The Wayne Brady Show* this afternoon? It's a variety show that's kid-friendly so I'm sure your group will really enjoy it. I can give you free tickets."

"Really?" I asked. "Are there any strings attached?"

"None whatsoever. Come be our special guests and plan to have a lot of fun."

He counted out the tickets, gave us a map

with directions to the studio, and told us what time to be there. The girls were excited by the unexpected turn of events.

Upon our arrival at the studio, the producer invited us backstage to meet the "Queen of Disco," singer-songwriter Donna Summer, who was the musical performer on the show that day. She gave each of the girls an autographed copy of her latest CD. The producer also asked the girls to open the show by introducing all the guests. We were then escorted to the front row, where we were treated like celebrities. Everybody was so happy.

As soon as the show was over, we raced back to our hotel to get ready for the evening. Seven females sharing two bathrooms made things interesting, but by the time we left for the gala, everybody looked beautiful and very grown up in their sparkly, long formal gowns.

We pulled up to the Hotel Casa del Mar in Santa Monica, where the gala was being held, and the place felt as magical as its name implied. The evening was starting to feel very surreal.

"My stomach feels a little funny, Mrs. Trull," Molly said. "I think it's because I'm getting nervous."

"Well, I think we're all a little excited, honey," I said, not wanting to let on that my stomach was a little queasy too.

Katie put her arm around Molly as we walked

in. "I promise that this is going to be a great evening. Just be yourself and enjoy the moment. You've all worked so hard and deserve this attention. Let's go have some fun!"

We found our way to the ballroom and were ushered to a special table. After a vegan dinner, the awards ceremony began. Actor John O'Hurley introduced actress Frances Fisher, who presented our award.

"The IDA nominating committee conducted a nationwide search to honor the young people of our country who best exemplify guardian-ship," Frances said. "All the nominees for the Distinguished Youth Guardian Award have demonstrated by example that animals are not to be treated as mere property, objects, or things, but as individuals with feelings, needs, and interests of their own. Among the many deserving entries, one nominee stood out for its landmark mission to start a no-kill sanctuary."

Frances went on to share the history of how our sanctuary began and that the IDA recognized our efforts in providing preventative care, including vaccinations, spaying, and neutering, to the homeless animals in Dalhart. Because of the kids' initiative in creating a no-kill shelter, IDA was hopeful that these youngsters would be representative of what the next generation would become.

When Frances ended her speech by introducing

us as the winners of the Youth Guardian Award, the seven of us wound our way through the maze of elegantly decorated tables up to the stage. We were greeted with a long round of applause from the audience and a standing ovation.

Frances ushered me to the podium and whispered that I should say a few words. My heart sank. I had no idea that I was going to have to make a speech; I was totally unprepared. I took a deep breath to still the nervousness that had suddenly bloomed in my chest, then I introduced all the girls and thanked the IDA for honoring us. I also shared the starfish story and how it applied to what my students were trying to accomplish. The audience seemed to love our story and gave us a second standing ovation when I finished my little speech.

Frances presented us with a large painting and a check for one thousand dollars. We got a third standing ovation as we headed back to our table.

After we were seated, John O'Hurley shared his thoughts about our efforts. "Isn't it inspiring to see children take the initiative? It gives you hope for the future. I find it so interesting that a bunch of kids who think locally and act locally can cause an effect that is global."

John went on to state that he believed the children would continue to do great things with their lives. And recognizing the significance of the evening, he also commented that they would remember this evening for the rest of their lives. I shared his sentiment completely.

Before leaving the gala, we had our pictures taken with Frances Fisher, John O'Hurley, and Pierce Brosnan. We also got to meet Dr. Goodall, who invited us to attend the filming of *Roots & Shoots* the next day. Roots & Shoots is a global youth-led community action program backed by the Jane Goodall Institute. It's composed of thousands of young people inspired by Dr. Goodall to make the world a better place.

Unfortunately, we had a flight out the next morning and had to graciously decline her invitation.

Heading back to our hotel, everyone was talking at once about what an amazing night it had been and how special everyone had made them feel. Some of the attendees even asked the girls for their autographs! I quickly discovered that driving in Los Angeles was a bit more challenging than driving in Dalhart. Vehicles zipped around at lightning speed, and there were endless roads to get lost on. In spite of the traffic maze coupled with the excitement of the evening, I thought I was doing a decent job maneuvering through the sprawling city. The flashing lights from a Los Angeles police car that pulled up behind me told me otherwise. I pulled over, and the police car followed suit. I watched in the rearview mirror as the policeman approached my window.

"Ma'am, may I ask where you're heading tonight?" the police officer politely asked.

"We've been attending a gala, where we were honored, and now I'm trying to get the group back to our hotel," I said. "Is there a problem, Officer?"

"Only a slight one," he said. "Are you aware that you've been driving in a designated bus lane?"

"No, I had no idea," I confessed. "Coming from a small town in Texas, I'm not used to driving in big cities. We don't have special bus lanes back home."

After checking my driver's license, he let me go with just a warning. "I'm not going to ruin your evening. Get these girls back safely and enjoy the rest of your night."

"Thank you so much, Officer. I'm sure we will." I was thrilled to be driving away without a traffic ticket as a souvenir. As we turned left at the next block, we passed a huge homeless shelter with people sitting outside in cardboard boxes. It had just started raining and the people looked so sad. It was such a stark difference from the place we had just left, one not lost on the young girls.

Kelsey said, "We really are blessed" and all the girls quietly agreed.

Despite getting an early start the next morning, we missed our flight back to Texas. The airline rerouted us on a later flight that took us through Las Vegas, Nevada. The downside was that we had a three-hour layover. Katie, being the ever-resourceful woman, managed to arrange a limousine tour of Las Vegas during our wait. The girls were beyond excited to add another first to their growing list of experiences from the trip.

WHEN I RETURNED to school on Monday, the principal asked to meet with me during lunch.

"Diane, I'm sorry to have to bring this up but the other teachers aren't really in support of the shelter or the kids' involvement with the dogs," she said.

"Really?" I asked incredulously. "All I can say is that I'm sorry if what we're doing has upset anybody. That was never our intent."

"Personally, I support what you are doing, and it has turned out to be a tremendous project for the kids. The teachers also don't like the fact that the proceeds from the recycling program you started aren't coming back to the school. They think the money should be spent on things like purchasing sports equipment for the students instead of feeding the dogs."

"Well, most of the classrooms aren't participating in the recycling program anyway, so I'm not sure why the teachers care where the money goes," I replied. "And because we have so few participants, the shelter has gotten less than one hundred fifty dollars since the program started. It's hardly enough to make a difference."

"I understand, Diane, I really do. I'm just trying to find a happy medium here. They've asked me to set up a meeting with you. Are you available after school today?"

I didn't know what to say. I still couldn't grasp why people were upset with what we were doing. Teachers, in particular, should understand the importance of teaching children about responsibility and compassion. The fact that innocent animals were benefitting from our efforts made it a double win. How could any of this be bad?

"Honestly, I'm not really sure what there is to talk about," I said. "I have a commitment at four o'clock today but I can meet another time. I promised my students that I would tape *The Wayne Brady Show* this afternoon so they could see themselves on television. I need to keep that promise. So, I guess my answer is no, I'm not available today."

My decision to miss the teachers' meeting caused a rift among the faculty. I was frustrated that the children's good intentions were being misconstrued by the adults. And apparently, the teachers were growing weary with my devotion to the kids and the shelter. I didn't know how to fix that with the teachers, but I became acutely aware of their concerns.

PART TWO

The greatness of a nation and its moral progress can be judged by the way its animals are treated.
—*MAHATMA GANDHI*

CHAPTER 9

Tears of Joy and Tears of Sorrow

■ ■ ■ ■ ■

Photo by Diane Trull

MOMMA DOG

Momma Dog came to DAWGS from a terrible hoarding situation in the small town of Hedley, Texas. Sweet Momma Dog was pregnant and very ill with distemper.

An amazing family fostered her and within two days of her arrival, the small dog delivered three precious babies. Sadly, none of the puppies survived and the hopes of Momma Dog being okay were very bleak.

Olivia, the foster family's precocious three-year-old daughter, decided Momma Dog needed her love and attention to get well. Every morning, Olivia greeted Momma Dog with a big hug and a morning song. She would then lay with the dog until her breakfast was ready. The afternoons were filled with naps for Momma Dog and treats that Olivia would sneak her. Most evenings Olivia was always found sleeping with her arm gently resting on Momma Dog's side, sharing a pillow.

Weeks went by before Momma Dog was better, but, by then, she had found her forever home with Olivia and her family.

■ ■ ■ ■ ■

THE BELL HAD JUST RUNG, signaling the end of the school day. I usually spent twenty minutes cleaning up my classroom, which gave the students time to go to their lockers and wrap up their day. Anybody needing a ride to the shelter knew to meet in my room. I don't think I ever left the school without a carload of children.

"We only have a few minutes before we leave, but there's something I want to discuss with everybody," I said after a handful of kids had trickled in.

"It's hard to believe but next month is the one-year anniversary since we opened DAWGS," I said. "I know it's been a struggle at times, but you've accomplished so much in such a short period of time. Incredibly, we've rescued more than nine hundred animals. I hope you all know how proud I am of you. To honor this special occasion, I think we should have some kind of celebration. While many have shown their support, I suspect there are those who didn't think we'd make it to this point. I want to include the community in our celebration. What would you think about the idea of hosting a dinner that's also a fundraiser?"

"Do you mean we'll have to sell tickets to get people to come?" Jesse asked. He sounded a little skeptical.

"A fundraiser can work in different ways," I explained. "In this case, we would sell tickets that would be considered a donation to the shelter. In return, we would provide dinner for those folks who bought tickets. I'm sure most of you have gone to the pre-game dinners that the high school hosts before some of the football and basketball games as a way to raise money. Our event would be very similar."

"I bet we could get a lot of people to come," Alix said. "Do you think we could have it in the school cafeteria?"

"I thought about that," I said. "We'll have to

check with Principal Coffman to see if she has any objections, but I don't think she will."

"What about having a silent auction like they did at the IDA gala?" Molly asked. "That might be a good way for us to raise extra money. Could we do something like that too?"

"That's a great idea, Molly," I said. "We can ask some of the local merchants to donate items or services and then our guests can bid on the ones they want to purchase. And the extra money that we make from the silent auction can be used to help fund our spay-and-neuter program. So, what does everybody think about the idea? It's something that we all need to agree on since it's going to require a lot of extra work from each of us."

"I like it, Mrs. Trull," Molly said, nodding her head. "It sounds like fun."

The rest of the group agreed.

"What kind of food are we going to have?" Jesse asked, sounding like a typical boy. "And what happens if a whole lot of people show up? How are we going to feed everybody?"

"Not knowing the exact number of people who might come can make things a bit tricky," I responded. "That's why we'll sell tickets in advance so we can get a close estimate of how much food we'll need. I think serving a spaghetti dinner might be the way to go, regardless of the number of folks who attend. It's easy to prepare and we can feed a lot of people with minimum effort.

"I'd also like for us to come up with a special name or theme for our event, so please be thinking about some possibilities. I know how clever you all are so come back with your best suggestions."

THE NEXT FEW weeks flew by as we prepared for our first official fundraiser. Once Principal Coffman approved our request to hold the event in the school cafeteria, we set the date for Saturday, March 6, 2004. Since we were planning to serve spaghetti, we named the event "The Lady and the Tramp Gala," in honor of the famous spaghetti scene in the Walt Disney movie *Lady and the Tramp*.

The local prison in Dalhart had a well-respected art program for its inmates. I contacted them about making two sets of life-sized wooden cutouts of the main characters in the movie, Lady, the cocker spaniel, and Tramp, the beloved stray mutt, as decorations for the dinner. We covered all the cafeteria tables with red construction paper and placed wine bottles dripped with candle wax as the centerpieces. I collected a bunch of large dead branches from the neighborhood and asked the kids to bring in strands of white Christmas lights from their homes. Katie and I decorated the limbs and placed them around the room.

The cafeteria was magically transformed into a charming Italian café!

Katie and two of her girlfriends offered to dish out the food, while my students volunteered to serve as the waitstaff. Linda, one of our very talented volunteers, offered to use her family recipe for making the spaghetti and spent days preparing the delicious special sauce and meatballs. The children decided it would be a good idea if all the volunteers dressed alike at the event, so we decided on a uniform of black pants and long-sleeved white shirts. To add a splash of color, the girls cut out big red hearts from thick construction paper, wrote each student's name on them in black magic marker, and pinned them to everyone's shirts before the event started.

As we were finishing up preparations on the day of the event, the mother of one of my students who was helping us pulled me aside. "Diane, I heard something this morning and I've been struggling about whether I should say anything to you," Donna said. "But the more I think about it, the more I think you should hear this.

"Apparently, the city has banned all of its employees from attending the gala tonight. I ran into one of my neighbors earlier this morning and I reminded him of the fundraiser. He told me that he wouldn't be able to make it because his boss had told him not to go. When I asked him why, he wouldn't elaborate, but he went on to say that all the city employees were told the same thing. If what he says is true, I don't know how that will affect the turnout, but I thought you would like to know ahead of time. Let's just hope he's wrong."

My heart sank, but I thanked Donna for letting me know. The city's attempt to sabotage our evening was one more concern I wish we didn't have to face. But because my students had put so much effort into planning the event, I said a quick prayer that the evening wouldn't be a total disaster.

Despite the threat of a boycott, we were pleasantly surprised by the turnout. More than three hundred people showed up to support our cause. During the evening, my students gave a presentation with photos of some of the dogs they had saved, just like they had at the city council meeting the year before. But unlike the cool reception they had received from the city council members, the gala's audience gave a standing ovation for their efforts.

Without a doubt, the silent auction was the highlight of the evening. We set up a room adjacent to the cafeteria where all the donated prizes were on display. The collection of items included roundtrip airline tickets from Amarillo to Houston as well as tickets to a Houston Rockets basketball game, a large-screen color television, and autographed posters from actor Ian McKellen, actress Sophia Loren, and entertainer

Jay Leno. But the most popular item turned out to be a side of beef, which generated a lot of money for the shelter. The evening ended with a live auction of one of our border collie puppies named Joby. In keeping with our adoption policy, we first conducted a home check to make sure the new owners could provide Joby with a safe and loving environment before releasing him to them.

The next morning, I was thinking about how the gala had exceeded my expectations when I received a frantic call from Cindy. She and another volunteer were at the sanctuary to start the morning feedings. When they'd gone into the puppy house, they'd made a gruesome discovery. The first thing the two women saw was one of the plastic baby gates we used to keep the litters separated lying on the floor and a lifeless, bloody body in the hallway.

"It was absolutely horrible," Cindy said to me, understandably shaken. "The puppy had been field dressed with slits that extended from his throat to his little belly. We have no way of knowing if the intruders killed the puppy before mutilating him, but, either way, I'm sure he died a miserable death."

I felt sick to my stomach listening to Cindy's news. I couldn't help but wonder if whoever did this wanted to shock the children by leaving the puppy's mangled body in plain view.

"Please don't say anything to the children about this," I asked her. "There's no reason to upset them. Give me five minutes to change my clothes and I'll be right over."

The rest of the day passed in a blur. Cindy and I were heartsick over what had happened, but we were determined to put on a brave face for the sake of the children.

BEFORE HEADING TO school the next morning, I decided to swing by the shelter to make sure everything was okay. The events from the previous day were still weighing heavy on my heart. When I pulled up to the front gate, something made me instantly uneasy. Although the chain and padlock were still securely wrapped around the front post as we had left it the night before, the metal gate had been shoved in as if somebody had tried to squeeze through the narrow opening without breaking the lock. If somebody had vandalized the shelter property, we would be able to deal with that, but my immediate concern was for the safety of all the animals in our care.

I unlocked the gate and checked on all the dogs in the outside kennels first. Although I didn't find anything amiss, my sixth sense was still on high alert. I decided to check on the puppies next. In the breath of a second, I knew something was terribly wrong. Two bloody bodies were in the same place where Cindy had found the dead puppy yesterday.

I knelt next to the lifeless puppies and saw that they, too, had been field dressed. What drives such hate I wondered as I looked at their mutilated bodies. The sacred space of our sanctuary felt violated. Trying to gather my emotions, I could hear the soft, gentle whimpering of other puppies coming from all the rooms and I went to check on everybody else. Fortunately, none of the other litters were harmed.

Every day, Mark and I face a multitude of challenges in running the shelter. From being positive mentors to the kids to operating on a shoestring budget, the struggles are real and ongoing. As difficult as all that can be, that's not the hardest part for us. Instead, it's dealing with the relatively small group of individuals who have lost their humanity and then trying to explain to the kids why people are like that, and that it's not okay to act that way. These horrific events made me even more determined to protect the children from learning about the atrocities.

After the break-ins, two elderly couples from the community volunteered to provide security watches at the shelter during the night. I was touched by their care and concern and hoped that the worst of these incidents were behind us.

Trying to focus on the positive, we were excited to welcome the Little Film Company to Dalhart the following week. The Little Film Company is a worldwide film sales and marketing company that distributes independent motion pictures. We had met Ellen, the owner, at the IDA gala. She had been instrumental in securing many of the silent auction items for our spaghetti dinner fundraiser. She also wanted to film a segment on our shelter that we could use for fundraising.

But the day that the film crew was scheduled to arrive, tragedy struck once again; this time while we were all in school. Cindy arrived at the shelter late in the morning to find eight dead golden puppies in the same place where we had found the other three. And just like before, these poor souls had been field dressed and left for the children to find.

Cindy managed to clean up the mess before the children and the film crew arrived in the afternoon. She also carefully and lovingly wrapped each of the puppies' bodies, preparing them for burial. We knew that we would have to tell the children that the puppies were dead. However, I was adamant that we spare them the ugly details of what really happened. Once everybody arrived at the shelter, we gathered the group together and told them that the puppies got sick and suddenly died.

"Did they have parvo?" Molly asked, sounding a little confused. "They all seemed fine yesterday."

"No, it was something else that came on quickly, and unfortunately, there was nothing we could do to save them," I explained, hoping that would satisfy the children's inquisitive minds.

"I know it's a bit of shock and that you'll miss playing with them. But sometimes things like this just happen and there's no real explanation."

"Can we bury these puppies with the other ones in the Little Angels Cemetery?" Jesse asked solemnly, after hearing the news.

"Yes, we can," I said as I reached out to tousle his hair. "In fact, I think we should have a ceremony before you start the afternoon feedings." My motive for wanting to bury the puppies right away was to avoid any of the children asking if they could see the puppies before we buried them.

Each of the children gently picked up one of the wrapped puppies along with their feed bucket and headed over to the cemetery. The children held hands, sobbed, and said prayers. Then they picked up their buckets and started their chores.

I so wished this was something the kids never had to see. But their spirits were resilient, and they were often the ones who taught Mark and me about forgiveness and staying the course.

"We really believe that dogs don't deserve to die if there's nothing wrong with them," the kids repeatedly told anybody who would listen. "To us, it just isn't right." That message soon became their mantra.

Despite the positive things we were accomplishing in our sanctuary, these heinous crimes reinforced the ongoing discord within the community. It was apparent the social climate of Dalhart remained divided. While there were many neighbors who supported and applauded our efforts, there were some people who believed it was wrong to teach children that the lives of animals were valuable, and they would go to great lengths to try to stop us.

Unfortunately, on days like this one, it seemed like the bad guys were winning. But perhaps what was more frustrating was that we didn't always know who was on which side.

While the children didn't seem fazed by the constant setbacks, there were times when it was difficult for me not to feel overwhelmed by all the negative distractions. Sometimes I would come home in tears and ask Mark, "What are we going to do?" And then, somehow, the next day would be a bit better. But often, it was the kids who kept us going. Mark and I recognized early on that the kids looked to us for leadership every single day and that the dogs depended on us for their lives. Once Mark and I had stepped into our roles, we knew we couldn't just walk away— because what would happen to all the dogs and how would that affect all the children?

After the golden puppies were killed, Mark filed a report with the local police. But without the luxury of having security cameras on the property, there were no leads to follow. Whoever killed the puppies had been masterful in ensuring no evidence was left behind. As hard as it was to believe, and much to my dismay, nobody was ever apprehended or even questioned. The horror of losing all those precious puppies still haunts me and the realization that someone would be so evil to innocent victims and had left that for the children to find is inconceivable.

In desperation, I called Ana Maria, a woman we had met as a result of the IDA gala in October. She had encouraged me to call her if we ever needed help. I hoped this qualified as one of those moments. When I told her what had happened to the puppies, she was appalled and generously gave us the funds to build a proper security fence around the entire property. She was hoping to ensure that something like this would never happen again. We were so grateful for her kindness, charitability, and compassion.

CHAPTER 10
Beauty Is in the
Eye of the Beholder

■ ■ ■ ■ ■

CHANCE

The game warden from our area found a very dirty dog, caked in mud and debris, wandering out in the country. Although he was sporting a weathered checkered bandana, he was miles away from any homes or farms. The game warden brought the dog to us.

After giving him a much-needed bath and brushing, we discovered a beautiful merle collie

133

we named Chance. He adored people and never acted like a dog—he would not lie down on the ground unless there was a blanket beneath him, and if there was furniture nearby, he always picked the nicest, most comfortable chair to sit in. He greeted everyone with his paw raised for a handshake or ready to give a "high five." It was obvious he once belonged to somebody who'd trained him and took care of him.

We had Chance at the sanctuary for several weeks hoping to find his missing family, but no one ever claimed him. We took him to an adoption event in Amarillo where a wonderful family saw him and instantly fell in love. Chance reciprocated that affection and today he is always with his family, whether going to work with his dad, playing with the kids or snuggling with his new mom.

■ ■ ■ ■ ■

A LOT GOES ON BEHIND THE SCENES of most animal rescue organizations. In addition to caring for a multitude of animals, many groups go the extra mile and monitor the activities of high-kill shelters in their areas as well. When an alert goes out that an animal has been placed on death row because its time has run out is when some of the best work of animal rescue kicks in. And although it may place an overwhelming burden on already-limited resources, most groups don't hesitate to say, "Yes, we can help," whenever an innocent animal is in need.

As space becomes available in our shelter, we often rescue animals that are moments away from being euthanized at other shelters. There are several rescue groups in Amarillo that we communicate with regularly. And although driving to Amarillo is nearly a two hundred-mile roundtrip journey for us, we've made countless trips at a moment's notice to pick up an animal that's on borrowed time.

One Saturday morning, I got an urgent call from one of the groups in Amarillo about one of their dogs that had severe skin issues. Sheldon was a large, older husky who was down to his last day. Despite his medical condition, the folks in Amarillo were anxious for somebody to claim him because of his exceptionally sweet nature. The timing was good as we had just adopted out several of our large dogs. As Cindy was helping with the morning feedings, I went looking for her to see if she would drive to Amarillo to rescue Sheldon.

I found her hosing down a stack of metal food bowls out in the shed. Several dogs were splashing through the puddles forming around her feet.

"Good morning, Cindy," I said. "Looks like you've got plenty of help this morning!"

"I sure do," Cindy replied as a smile spread across her face.

"I just found out that Amarillo has a senior dog that is down to his final hours. Do you have time to head over there today and pick him up for us? If so, I'll call to tell them to put a hold on him and that you'll be there in a few hours."

"You bet I do!" she said. "I'll ask Kat to finish the morning feedings so I can leave within the hour."

Kathryn, or Kat as everybody lovingly called her, was becoming one of our most valuable resources. Kat and Katie knew each other from middle school but it wasn't until Katie returned home from college to assist us with running the sanctuary that their friendship developed. Katie had invited Kat to come to the shelter one afternoon to help photograph some of the dogs so we could post their pictures on social media websites, including www.petfinder.com and www.Adopt-a-Pet.com. (Petfinder.com is a searchable online database in which nearly 11,000 animal shelters and adoption organizations across the US, Canada, and Mexico post their adoptable pets' photos and profiles. Adopt-a-Pet.com is North America's largest non-profit pet adoption website that helps more than 17,000 animal shelters, humane societies, SPCAs, pet rescue groups, and pet adoption agencies advertise their homeless pets to millions of adopters a month, for free.) Both sites have helped broaden our adoption base dramatically by giving people around the country exposure to our dogs. Keeping an updated listing of our available dogs on myriad social media sites is critical in helping them find new homes. I remember Kat telling me how overwhelmed she felt after her first visit, but at the same time how drawn she was to the work that we were doing.

She started showing up at the shelter a few days a week to help with odd jobs and developed a keen interest in how medicine was used in caring for the sick and injured animals. With guidance from Cindy, Katie and Kat learned how to administer vaccinations, draw blood, and check for parasites. They were often on the front lines in caring for many of our ill and injured rescues.

Cindy and Kat were a formidable team and I was grateful for their dedication to our shelter.

I was in the office going through my e-mails when Cindy got back late in the day.

"Hey, Diane, how's it going?" Cindy asked.

She seemed to be cautiously peeking her head around the door. I immediately knew that something was up. Cindy was rarely tentative.

"I'm fine," I said. "Did you have any problems in getting Sheldon?"

"Nope, no issues at all," she said, still halfway hiding behind the door. "The kids are already getting him settled in. He's a little shy at first, but

I don't think we'll have any trouble finding him a good home when it's time. He seems like a really sweet dog. A little extra love and care should cure him."

"Great. So, if things are fine with Sheldon, why do I get the funny feeling there's something else going on?"

Cindy nodded a few times, almost as if she was carrying on some internal conversation. She seemed to be rallying her courage. And then she spoke.

"Well, Diane, you know what a sucker I am for a sweet face, so promise me you won't be mad but there was this little Pomeranian in quarantine and my heart broke when I saw her," she said, her words coming out in a rush. "I know finances are tight right now and that bringing in a dog with major medical problems isn't ideal, but she's such a cutie-pie. She deserves better than being left to die on a cold concrete floor. After I had filled out the adoption papers for Sheldon and loaded him in my truck, I couldn't stop thinking about Carmella and her fate if she was left behind. I drove back to the facility and rescued her, too."

She finally stepped out from behind the door and led an orange-and-white ball of fluff on a leash. The little dog started yelping and wiggling as soon as she saw me. Although she looked a bit frail, she had a lot of spirit.

"This is Carmella," Cindy continued. "The staff at the shelter said she has a cancerous tumor in her stomach and that she doesn't have long to live. Even if she's as sick as they say she is, I know we can love her and make her last days as comfortable as possible."

I reached down to pet Carmella. "Hello, pretty little girl," I said. Her sweet, eager face looked up at me. I melted.

"Oh, I probably would have done the same thing, Cindy," I said. "Carmella needs to be here with us. I'll make an appointment to take her to the veterinarian and get a second opinion. We'll figure something out."

A few days later I saw Cindy at the shelter and I couldn't wait to tell her the good news. Instead of having stomach cancer, Carmella had been diagnosed with a hernia that was completely treatable with surgery. The veterinarian predicted that she would make a full recovery.

"I have no doubt that once Carmella is healed and ready to head out to the adoption events, somebody will scoop her and that squeaky little bark up in no time." I smiled at Cindy. "I'm so glad you brought her back here so we can make sure she gets a second chance at a good life."

WITHOUT A DOUBT, the weather in the Texas Panhandle remains one of our biggest challenges. In spring, there are torrential rains, hailstorms, and powerful windstorms. Summer brings suffocating heat and relentless humidity. Fall brings more rain and wind and the occasional tornado. And then comes winter, with its snow and frigid temperatures. Although the seasons differ widely, the battle in dealing with the different elements remains constant.

The rainy season had begun, and Mark and I got home later than normal one night after making the final rounds at the shelter. Widespread thunderstorms had developed in the area during the afternoon, which slowed our progress. The wind was howling outside, and I was glad to be safely tucked in for the night.

Around eleven o'clock, Mark got a call from one of the neighbors who lived near the shelter. One of our metal storage sheds had blown over the ten-foot-high perimeter fence. Even though we had anchored it with sand bags, the wind was so strong it flipped the shed over the fence. It landed on the road that runs next to the shelter and was partially blocking it. Because the road isn't traveled much, especially at night, Mark thanked the man for calling and said he would move the shed the next day.

Mark went to work in the morning, but when he got another call about the shed, he left work early and headed to the shelter. I got a call from him a few hours later.

"Well, this has turned out to be an interesting

day," he said when I answered the phone. "I parked my truck next to where the shed had landed and was trying to figure out the best way to move it. A different neighbor from the one who called last night came driving down the road. When he stopped and got out of his car, I thought he might offer his help with moving the shed.

"Instead, he started yelling and screaming and told me that I'm going to hell because of the dogs we're trying to save. It was the craziest thing! I kept telling him to calm down but the more I said that, the madder he seemed to get. I realized there was no way to talk to him rationally, so I went about my business and ignored him. He finally drove away.

"However, the real reason I'm calling is to let you know that when the shed blew over it pulled some of the fence down with it and apparently Hooch and Cheyenne got loose. Some of my coworkers are helping me move the shed now and then we're going to start looking for the dogs."

My heart sank when I heard Mark's news. I told him I would be there as soon as school was over.

By the time I got to the shelter, Hooch had returned on his own, but Cheyenne was still missing. I grabbed some students and hopped in my truck and started scouring the area. We found Cheyenne in a field down the road. Apparently, she had been hit by a car. I couldn't help but wonder if the neighbor who had been screaming at Mark earlier in the day was the one who'd hit her. Cheyenne was in pretty bad shape, but the worst was her beautiful tail. It had been severely cut and would need to be amputated. She had to spend a week at the vet. Hooch and the students had really missed her.

Knowing my family was being unfairly attacked because of their efforts to help my students fulfill their dream weighed on me like bricks. When we first set up the shelter, I painted a message on one of the interior walls of the barn. I wanted everybody who spent time there to have a visual reminder every day of our mission principles.

Remember
    Perseverance
    Determination
    Sense of Responsibility

But mostly
    Caring and Compassion
    For All

Sadly, I wasn't feeling very compassionate toward our neighbors at that moment.

CHAPTER 11

A Christmas Miracle

■ ■ ■ ■ ■

Photo by Diane Trull

BOB

Bob was a beautiful white and orange tabby cat that was surrendered to us after being viciously attacked by a dog. Bob was unable to move his back legs and kept crying with the most pitiful of meows. We took him to our veterinarian who told us that with medicine, bedrest, and lots of prayers he might make it.

With the help of one of our young volunteers, Rachel, Bob quickly recovered and thrived with all the attention he received. After several months, he was finally able to go to adoptions.

Bob quickly won the hearts of a nice family and went to his forever home where they think he is the best cat ever. He loves his new family and is often found sunning himself in the kitchen nook.

■ ■ ■ ■ ■

HOLIDAYS AREN'T DIFFERENT from any other day at the sanctuary. Although we had weathered severe winters before, December 2004 was exceptionally brutal, even by Texas Panhandle standards. The trees had been swept bare and snow was falling in huge, soft flakes, carpeting the roads, our heads, and all the animals. The forecast was grim with several more feet of white powder coupled with freezing fog predicted, which would bring the simplest of activities to an icy halt.

The wintry weather reminded me of a scene from the classic television movie *Rudolph, the Red-Nosed Reindeer* when Yukon Cornelius, the loveable prospector who shows up in Christmas Town after capturing the abominable snowman, exclaims, "Open up! It isn't a fit night out for man nor beast."

But regardless of what Mother Nature was

dishing out, we still had to care for our dogs.

It was bitterly cold two days before Christmas. Winds dropped the temperature to a bone-chilling minus fourteen degrees Fahrenheit. It was almost painful to breathe. We were frantic to make sure all of our animals survived the next several days. We had our work cut out for us.

After giving everyone their work assignments for the morning, I headed out to the nearest row of kennels to start breaking up the ice in the metal water buckets. I knew it was a futile exercise since the water would quickly freeze over again, but I wanted to make sure the dogs had access to drinking water, even if it was only for a few hours. Plus, I wanted to keep an eye on the children who were working outside to make sure they were taking proper breaks to go inside and warm up.

"I could use some help over here," Alix said, waving a small pitchfork in the air with her gloved hands. She was standing next to the kennels where I was working, and her breath came out in white, frosty puffs against the cold air.

Molly, who was wrapped from head to toe in winter clothing and heavy snow boots, did her best to run over to Alix. "What are you trying to do?" she asked, looking at the hay bales surrounding them.

"Mr. Trull said we need to spread some hay into

each of the kennels so it will soak up the snow," Alix said. "I want to make sure we put enough down where it's nice and thick so the dogs can curl up in it and stay warm."

Molly picked up a shovel and started tossing hay into the yellow plastic wheelbarrow. The two girls worked side by side in a comfortable rhythm.

"So, what do you think you're going to get for Christmas?" I heard Alix ask Molly.

"What do I think I'm going to get or what do I hope I'm going to get? Unfortunately, there's a really big difference between the two."

"Well, aside from wanting your own dog, what else do you want?" Alix asked.

"Are you serious?" Molly asked. She plunged the pitchfork into the bale of hay and looked at her friend, disbelievingly. "You know that's all I want. How long have I talked about wanting to have a pet of my own? But since we started DAWGS, my mom doesn't think we need to get one. She thinks that with all the dogs here in the shelter, I have more than enough animals to care for."

Molly yanked the pitchfork out from the bale and started shoveling again. "But it's not the same," she bemoaned. "As much as I love taking care of all the shelter dogs, I want one special dog that I can love and spoil and be with when I'm not here. I want my very own dog."

"Well, who knows? Maybe your mom will surprise you one day," Alix said.

When the wheelbarrow was overflowing with hay, each girl grabbed one of the wooden handles, and together they slowly pushed it forward.

I watched as they struggled to keep it upright as they trudged through the snow heading to the next row of kennels. And once again I was struck by their dedication. Instead of making snow angels or staying indoors drinking hot chocolate, these two precious girls were putting their comfort aside for the sake of helping the animals. Their commitment was inspiring.

The arrival of the heavy snows couldn't have come at a worse time. We were running out of money, which also meant we were running out of food. The city's promise to give us a monthly stipend had lasted only two months. Similarly, when we initiated the recycling program, our hope was that it would serve as a steady source of supplemental income for us. Although the city netted thousands of dollars from our efforts, they determined our share. As a result, we received only one check from them in the amount of one hundred thirty-eight dollars. Hardly enough to make a difference when you're trying to feed hundreds of hungry mouths.

I called around to several of the local pet stores asking for help. One of the stores generously donated two pallets of canned dog food. Although we were extremely grateful for the food, we now had a problem of a different magnitude.

With more than two hundred and fifty dogs in our care, we usually go through about three hundred pounds of food every day. Our usual protocol is to feed the dogs dry food since it's easier to store the large bags and we can make the rounds a lot faster. With canned food, each one must be opened by hand—one can at a time—making it a less-than-ideal way to feed the entire sanctuary. (Senior dogs, pregnant dogs, or dogs recovering from illnesses or surgeries are the exception. We feed them canned food because they need the extra calories.) But we were not about to look a gift horse in the mouth. Several of the kids went home and brought their electric can openers and got busy opening the mountain of seven hundred cans.

"I bet I can open more cans faster than you," the kids challenged each other as they took turns inside the barn to warm up. It soon became a contest the kids were clearly enjoying. The constant hum of the can openers provided a comforting backdrop for all the giggling and laughter echoing throughout the building.

Six hours and three burned-out can openers later, we were ready to start feeding the animals.

"Let's get an assembly line going," Molly suggested. Her organizational skills were clearly coming into focus. "The food bowls should go on one end of the counter and the opened cans at the other end. If we line up the wheelbarrows at the very end, we can stack the filled bowls in them and start heading out to the kennels. But make sure that you dump two cans of food into each bowl. It's really cold out there and the dogs need the extra food. And be sure to wish each of the dogs an early 'Merry Christmas'!"

Molly's plan was working like a charm. As each wheelbarrow was filled, the kids ventured out in pairs. Jesse and his sister Alicia were the first in line.

"We'll take care of feeding all the puppies," Jesse announced to the others.

The small building housing all the pregnant dogs and puppies was filled to capacity. There was a total of seventy-two puppies and their moms in that building alone. The rest of the children took care of feeding the dogs in the outside kennels.

The freezing weather also wreaked havoc on our water supply. When the temperatures plummeted, the pump in our water well often went out and the water pipes would freeze and burst, leaving us with no running water. Since we couldn't operate without water, we would fill a five-hundred-gallon water tank and haul it around the shelter on the back of a pickup truck. A handful of volunteers would go out ahead of the tank and chisel the ice out of the water buckets in each of the kennels, then the group behind them would drag the tank and refill the water bowls. There were a few days when it was so cold that the water tank froze, forcing us to buy plastic water jugs and go back and forth refilling them at a nearby home.

Between the extra time it took to manually open all the cans of food and refill each of the water buckets, it was eleven at night before we finished making all the rounds.

"Yes, we did it!" Jesse exclaimed as he rolled the last wheelbarrow back into the barn. "Every single dog is warm, fed, watered, and safe for another night."

We were absolutely exhausted but thrilled with our accomplishments.

The next morning, December 24, was even colder. With the wind chill, the temperature had dipped to an unbearable minus twenty-two. It was the worst of Dalhart's winter days. Mark and I were in the car inching our way through the snow along the slippery gray road to pick up some torn bags of dog food that a local supplier had generously donated. A ride that usually took five minutes stretched to one hour due to the fine layer of ice coating the roads. When we finally made it back to town, we picked up a small band of volunteers from their homes, making sure everybody was bundled up in their warmest clothes, masks, and insulated gloves.

"What's that by the front gate?" Alix said pointing to something when we finally arrived at the shelter. The falling snow swirled in a whirlwind around the truck, making it hard to see. From the driveway, all we could make out were two dark shapes.

The kids jumped out and trudged over to the fence. The icy snow crunched beneath their feet. The two dark shapes turned out to be two female black Labrador mixes. Both had yellow rope around their necks and were tied to the fence on very short leads.

Before leaving the shelter every night, the children leave bowls of food and water by the gate for any stray dogs that wandered by. These two beauties had been tied more than twenty feet away from those bowls.

I'm not sure what makes people think it's okay to anonymously leave their pet at our doorstep instead of surrendering them properly. And to abandon an animal during horrific weather conditions is even harder to comprehend. I suspect it must be guilt, but whatever the reason, sadly, this wasn't the first time that a dog was left at our shelter after hours.

As we slowly approached the gate, the dogs whimpered and wagged their tails. The snow was flying off their wiggling bodies.

"It's okay," Jesse murmured quietly. "We're not going to hurt you. You're safe now." He knelt in the snow and gently petted them. "I can't believe somebody just dumped them here in the middle of this terrible storm. It's so cruel."

The dogs weren't much more than puppies themselves, maybe seven or eight months old. And both were extremely pregnant.

"Come on. We've got to get these dogs inside where it's warmer," Alix urged. She already had the ropes untied and was leading the dogs toward the gate.

I wasn't sure where we were going to put these new arrivals—the puppy house was already overflowing—but, without a doubt, these two had to be indoors.

We hurried them into the small building. Once inside, we dried them off with towels and gave them food and water. A small space heater provided welcomed heat to the dogs and us.

Using expandable baby gates, the kids moved two litters of weaned puppies from one of the rooms into the hallway so we could use the vacant room for our new arrivals.

"Jesse and Molly, will you please bring in two more wading pools and make sure they're cleaned and sanitized?" I asked. "Alix, Kali and Lauren, will you help me mop up the floors in here and bring in some fresh bedding?"

Having experienced firsthand the devastating effects of parvo on puppies, we took an abundance of precaution when preparing the areas where new litters were born. Thorough cleanliness within the first few weeks of a puppy's life greatly reduces the spread of the potentially life-threatening parvo bacteria. Through trial and error, we also discovered that a little kiddie wading pool works perfectly as a nesting box for newborns. They can't climb out of them and the pools can be easily cleaned and sanitized.

"So, what should we name these two dogs?" I asked the girls as we were getting the room set up.

"Since it's almost Christmas, it needs to be something Christmassy," Alix said.

"What about naming them after some of Santa's reindeer?" Lauren offered. "Something like Dancer and Prancer?"

"Nah, I don't like that. It should be something more special," Kali shared.

"Okay, how about Mistletoe and Holly?" Lauren suggested. "That's pretty Christmassy."

"That's better, but still not quite right," said Alix.

The girls remained deep in thought as we continued cleaning the room.

"I know," Alix said. "Since they were abandoned on one of the coldest nights and we're able to offer them shelter, I think we should name them Mary and Maria."

Nodding their heads, Lauren and Kali agreed.

"I think those are perfect names," I said. "And

since the room is now clean and ready, why don't you bring Mary and Maria in and let's see how they like their new home?"

After sniffing around the room, the two dogs curled up on their soft beds.

"I think they are going to be very happy here," Lauren said.

"Let's leave Mary and Maria alone for a bit so they can take a nap and rest up," I said. "They've got a big job ahead of them."

As we turned to walk out of the room, Alix walked back over to the dogs and squatted down between them. "Merry Christmas, Mary," she softly said. "Merry Christmas, Maria." After giving each dog a gentle kiss on their heads, she stood up and walked out with us.

Christmas morning was a present in and of itself. The snow had mercifully stopped and the sky was a brilliant blue. The winter sunshine bounced off the snow-capped tree branches.

Mark and I got up early and headed to the shelter to make sure everybody had made it through the night safely. We entered the puppy house and could hear a multitude of soft whimpers coming from down the hall. Looking in on our newest residents, we discovered that overnight both Mary and Maria had given birth. In a few short hours, the DAWGS' puppy population had increased by seventeen!

We cleaned up all the dogs and their beds and

stood for a moment to marvel at the wonderful gift of life. The previous few days had been so challenging with the snow and the lack of food and water. Then, unexpectedly, we were given the precious gift of these two new mommas and their sweet little babies.

Every animal's life we've saved is worth celebrating but saving these two families on Christmas Eve felt extra special.

CHAPTER 12
Fighting City Hall
■ ■ ■ ■ ■

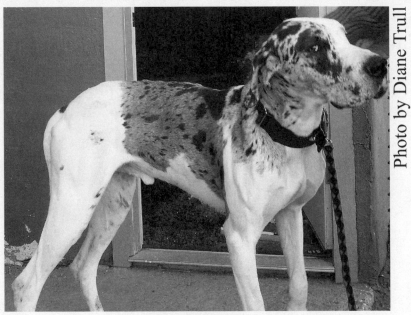

Photo by Diane Trull

BENTLEY

Bentley was a very large and loveable Great Dane. When we saw him galloping across a wheat field out in the middle of nowhere, we knew something was wrong. After hours of trying to catch him, he finally gave up, laid down, and let us bring him back to the sanctuary.

After successfully locating his family, they told us they had been traveling through town when Bentley got away from them. They also told us they weren't interested in coming back for him.

We had Bentley for only a few weeks when a wonderful family from Kansas came and adopted him. He is now happy in his new forever home.

■ ■ ■ ■ ■

I IMAGINE THAT MOST TAXPAYERS aren't aware of the expenses it takes to maintain an animal control department. In Dalhart, like most other places, taxpayers shoulder the cost of the animal control agent's salary, his or her vehicle, fuel for the vehicle, and a facility to house the animals for the required three-day holding period. And for every dog at Dalhart Animal Control that does not get claimed, the city pays ten dollars to have the animal euthanized.

As was common knowledge by now, the city had been euthanizing hundreds of dogs every year. Due to the students' dedication and determination to save as many animals as possible, Dalhart's annual euthanasia rate plummeted from six hundred dogs to around seventy. Since our founding two years ago, we had taken in more than three thousand healthy dogs that would have been euthanized before the city's pound became a no-kill facility.

In addition to the money saved from the reduction of euthanasia fees, the operating costs of the animal control facility were also trimmed because the city was housing fewer animals on average, which, in turn, reduced the amount of food needed to feed them.

It doesn't take an advanced degree in mathematics to understand that our modest shelter was saving the city money. A lot of money. But despite the benefits we were providing, we were hearing nasty rumors that the city was thinking about asking us to give them back their land.

So, once again, Mark and I found ourselves defending our actions and our shelter at the monthly city council meeting.

"From the very beginning, our focus has been to create a sense of awareness within our community regarding the stray dogs," I reminded the council members. "Dalhart's dog problem is still out of control and we want to keep the focus on personal responsibility when it comes to owning pets. The number of dogs we take in has always been a concern. Just last June and July, we had approximately one hundred dogs dropped off to us.

"While many of the dogs we care for are brought to us by animal control, the majority are surrendered by their owners. Unfortunately, we have an incredibly high number of citizens who believe it's their right to have a dog until it becomes an inconvenience to their lifestyle. It's very hard to teach children about compassion and responsibility when they see adults treating animals as temporary and disposable and acting irresponsibly toward their care.

"It's very rare that we adopt out locally. Because of Dalhart's small population and geographical isolation, we're trying to move the animals out of town, not just recycle them within the community. We've started networking with groups in other states, including Colorado, New Mexico, Oklahoma, Arizona, Utah, Florida, New York, Pennsylvania, and of course, other cities in Texas. Because of these affiliations, more than ninety percent of our adoptions are now out of state. Just last month, we flew sixteen of our puppies to New York to be adopted. It's hard to believe there are some areas of the country that don't have enough healthy dogs available for adoption. The dogs that we're transporting around the country would have been destroyed if our shelter didn't exist. Now, they are getting a second chance to become someone's best friend.

"While some people may think it's inhumane to keep dogs in a shelter, Mark and I believe it's inhumane for a community to allow hundreds of puppies to be born each year in abandoned buildings and empty fields. As these puppies grow up, they will typically eat out of trash cans and become ill from disease, which can cause a public health issue. And eventually, the breeding cycle starts all over again, unless they get hit by a vehicle and crawl off and die a miserable death somewhere. It's a staggering statistic, but a single female dog can be responsible for adding sixty-seven thousand puppies to the population over a six-year period.

"We've heard rumblings that some people think Dalhart should go back to euthanizing the dogs as a means of solving the overpopulation problem. But if my memory serves me correctly, when Dalhart was euthanizing hundreds of dogs every year, we had a major problem with too many stray dogs roaming the streets. The choice shouldn't be between whether we euthanize our stray population or keep them in shelters until they can find a new home. Those options only address the symptom and not the disease. The disease is chronic irresponsibility on the part of a lot of dog owners in Dalhart. And, as a community, we have a responsibility to educate the public on the benefits of spaying or neutering their pets.

"This problem isn't unique to our town. Many cities throughout the United States have taken the necessary steps to fix their animal problems, and they have seen remarkable results. Colorado fines its residents two hundred dollars if their pets aren't spayed or neutered. And as we know, they now must transport dogs into their state to keep up with adoption demands. This problem has been with us for many years, and therefore, the solution will not come easily. We firmly believe that with the help from our community leaders and the desire of our citizens to take responsibility, we will one day be able to walk our streets and enjoy our parks without having to be afraid of loose dogs.

"Believe it or not, we hope there comes a day when our facility is no longer needed. If that were to happen, that would mean we were successful in changing people's mind-sets about caring for companion animals."

The mayor closed his eyes and pinched the bridge of his nose between his thumb and forefinger. I wasn't sure if my passionate speech was giving him a headache or if he was simply counting to ten to gain his composure before replying.

When the mayor still didn't say anything, Mark chimed in. "We've always understood that our current location by the city cemetery isn't permanent. And we understand that people living in the area are tired of the barking. If we can get the dog population down at the shelter, we can then spread the dogs around better on the property, which will minimize the barking.

"Alternatively, if there's a larger piece of land that we can move to, that would help considerably. At one time, there was mention of some city-owned land between the airport and the prison that could potentially be a site for us. Diane and I have gone out there several times, and we believe it's a good option for us. It's far enough away from any residents and there is ample space to accommodate the large number of animals currently in our care."

The property Mark was referring to was the former Dalhart Army Airfield, which had served as a training site during World War II. Four large hangars, along with support buildings and barracks, had once dotted the property. Electric, sewer, and water lines were constructed in 1942. Today, the concrete pads where the buildings sat were the only remnants of the air base. The property had been vacant since the end of the war. It would be perfect for our needs.

"Well, some residents have expressed concern about the potential noise, lights, and smell if we donate that land to you," the mayor said. "In addition, there are obvious safety concerns. It would only take one dog running loose on the runway and then we'd all have a much bigger problem on our hands."

"How many people have complained?" Mark asked.

"Oh, I'm not sure of the exact number, but it was several folks," the mayor said, looking displeased.

"How many is several?"

"Well, it was a few, but we're not at liberty to disclose who those individuals are."

Realizing it was a futile discussion, Mark changed topics.

"Diane and I have been approached by a private foundation out of Amarillo that is willing to fund the construction of a new building, but that foundation insists that the city be part of the shelter project, too. They want the shelter and the community to work together to keep the dog population under control, and I'm okay with that. Our focus has always been to create a sense of awareness in the community regarding the dog problem.

"We believe the land by the airport would be a good choice. The foundation asked us to get a preliminary design drawn up, which we've done. The new facility would enable the dogs to be outside between the hours of eight in the morning and five at night. Two security fences would surround the facility, preventing dogs from escaping. The chance of a dog being loose on the runway is extremely remote. The current animal control building is located next to the runway and there has never been any issues with the dogs escaping and being a problem. Any noise the dogs make would be canceled out by the sounds of planes taking off and landing. And with the thousands of cattle on feedlots within a two-mile radius of the airport, I hardly think the smells or the barking being generated from our shelter would be a problem."

The mayor wasn't budging. "Well, it's just not something we're willing to take a risk on. No one is against your project, Mark. The sanctuary has been a definite benefit to the city. But we've looked at all the property that the city owns and, unfortunately, we just don't have any other land available."

Mark and I had heard from several sources that the city was in conversation with a local feed company about establishing a rail spur near the feed company's warehouse. This would enable the company, which was located near the shelter, to have direct access to the railroad tracks for shipping their grain instead of offloading the grain onto one rail and then moving it to another rail. The proposed spur would run straight through the shelter.

"We've heard that the city might want the property back where our shelter sits because of a railroad spur," I said. "Will you please address that rumor for us?"

"Contrary to what you may have heard, the shelter's size and the excessive barking are the only concerns we have with your project," the city manager said. "While the proposed spur to the animal feed plant would go near the shelter, none of the city's land would be used for it. The acreage that the shelter currently sits on was deeded to the city for water-well development years ago. It may go back to being used for cattle grazing at some point in the future."

It was obvious we had reached a stalemate, and the frustration that emanated from both sides of the table was palpable. The meeting ended without resolution.

"This is absolutely mind-boggling," Mark said to me as we left the building. "Cities will usually say, 'Okay, here are ten or twenty acres. That's our commitment.' When we first started the shelter, we were very conscious of trying not to put any financial burden on the city. But for them to refuse to jointly participate in our plans outright, especially when we have third-party funding, is absurd. I really don't get it."

"I wonder if this battle will ever end," I sighed. The weariness of constantly having to defend ourselves was weighing heavily on my heart. I closed my eyes, just for a moment. "I believe that the city is feeding off the public complaints against the shelter that have been based either on intentional misinformation or lack of information. For all the good that we're accomplishing, it shouldn't be this hard to find a way to work together."

A FEW WEEKS later we learned that the residents who had lobbied against relocating our shelter out by the airport signed an agreement with the city allowing them to move the shooting range to the same piece of property. It was hard to believe that people thought the sound of gunshots in their neighborhood would be less objectionable than some barking dogs.

CHAPTER 13

A Star Is Born

■ ■ ■ ■ ■

Photo by Diane Trull

TEDDY

Teddy was one of those dogs waiting for some-one special to find him. He came to us from a kill shelter in Texhoma, Oklahoma, and we cared for him for almost a year. He was a beautiful golden mix and was extremely friendly with everyone. During one of our mobile adoptions in Amarillo, a very nice woman was looking for a special dog to help at the children's hospital and to go with her on visits to the veterans' home. There was something about Teddy that caught her eye.

167

She adopted him, took him home, and today Teddy is an excellent therapy dog. He loves to visit people and will softly lay his head on any welcoming lap to offer unconditional love in return for a gentle pat on the head.

■ ■ ■ ■ ■

THERE WERE NUMEROUS TIMES when I felt that life at the shelter had become a living laboratory demonstrating English mathematician Sir Isaac Newton's third law of motion: for every action, there is an equal and opposite reaction. In contrast to the constant barrage of negativity we faced from the city, there was almost always an equal number of amazing people who came our way, people who were genuinely concerned about the animals and were willing to go the extra mile (sometimes literally) to help them. And it's through these kindhearted individuals that many dogs came into our care.

Winter had finally released its frigid grip and spring was once again in full bloom throughout the Panhandle. Wildflowers exploded across the green landscape in a tumble of color, and the dogs were happy to roll in any patch of warm sunshine they could find. It was hard to believe that we would soon be dealing with the dog days of summer again.

The kids had just arrived at the shelter after finishing their day at school. Alix was the first to spot the young couple. "Mrs. Trull, it looks like we have some visitors."

The man and woman had parked close to the gate and were trying to coax three medium-sized, tan border terriers from their car. My heart sank. Were they giving up their family pets? We were almost at full capacity. Spring is prime breeding season so we were already overflowing with the number of mouths we had to feed. But regardless of what brings a person to our shelter, I always advocate that we must be polite to everybody. It's too easy to pass judgment when somebody relinquishes their pet to us, and the reality is that we don't ever know a person's full story.

I walked out through the front gate and ushered in the visitors. "Hi, welcome to DAWGS," I said, extending my hand to the woman. "I'm Diane and this is Alix, one of my helpers. Seeing that you've got your hands full, I'm assuming you're not here to adopt any dogs, are you?"

"Unfortunately, no," the woman replied. "We already have two dogs at home, but we want to help these three in any way we can."

Alix bent down to pet the dogs and they seemed happy to have her attention. "They seem really well behaved and they look like they're in pretty good shape," Alix said. "Where did they come from?"

"My husband and I were running errands and stopped at the drugstore," the woman explained.

"We were walking to the car to leave when Steve thought he heard a dog whimpering. Looking around we didn't see anything. But as we kept walking, the whimpering continued. It seemed as if the sound was coming from the trash dumpster at the edge of the parking lot."

Steve continued the story. "We lifted the lid of the dumpster and peered in. We were shocked to see not one, but three little faces looking up at us. It was so smelly and dirty in there. The dogs were cowering a bit, but they seemed to understand that we were there to help them. How on earth can a person throw away an animal?"

I nodded. "Based on the condition of some of the animals that arrive here at the shelter, that's a question we find ourselves asking a lot. It's hard to comprehend how poorly humanity behaves sometimes."

Alix stood up from petting the new arrivals. "Well, believe it or not, we've had people who have come to the shelter and said, 'Take this dog or I'm going to shoot it.' Sometimes we want to say to them, 'You're the reason we have to have the shelter. You don't know how to take care of your pets.' But Mrs. Trull won't let us say that. I can't understand why people won't take care of their pets. It would be so simple if they had them spayed and neutered. Then there wouldn't be so many dogs that need homes."

The couple seemed almost apologetic for not

being able to keep the dogs themselves, but I assured them that they would be in good hands. Just then Jenna, Sarah, and Sadye came around the corner and the four girls took the dogs to an empty pen and got them fed. They looked so comfortable laying on their blankets and chewing on their treats.

Before leaving, the couple handed me a small donation, which I'm sure was money that would have served them better elsewhere. But sensing that they were true animal lovers, I graciously thanked them for all they had done.

The children named our newest arrivals Angela, Toby, and Olivia. It looked like they were siblings, and we estimated they were less than a year old. Although they were a bit scared at first, the trio settled in and quickly became part of the DAWGS family.

A few months later, I got a phone call from Debra Coe of Coe's Animal Talent, Inc., an animal talent agency in Canada. Debra had spotted Angela's picture on www.petfinders.com and she wanted more information on her.

"I'm scouting for several similar-looking dogs to play the leading role of Lucky in the next *Dr. Dolittle* sequel," Debra explained. "*Dr. Dolittle 3* will be a direct-to-video production that chronicles the tales of a young woman who inherits her veterinarian father's amazing gift of talking to animals. The role of

Lucky was previously played by another dog, but after two movies, that original dog is getting too old to continue the part."

Over the next few weeks, Debra and I had several conversations about Angela's behavior, temperament, and personality. I sent Angela's health records to Debra as well as pictures and videos of the kids playing with her. Angela had a sweet disposition and loved being the center of attention. She also got along well with other animals.

"Because we're not looking for a purebred, it's a little more difficult searching around North America for a particular kind of mutt," Debra said. "We have to find the same capabilities and characteristics in several dogs that are roughly the same age, size, and color."

It didn't take long for Debra to decide that Angela would be perfect for the role. And just like that, Angela was adopted over the phone.

It took several more weeks before the arrangements were finalized for me to fly Angela to Vancouver, Canada, where she would live. Debra mailed me a special harness and cushion that allowed Angela to fly celebrity status inside the cabin of the plane rather than in the cargo hold. The flight attendants and passengers made quite a fuss over her. It was a happy moment when I handed Angela to Debra, knowing that she had a great life ahead of her.

Flying back home to Dalhart the next day, I couldn't help but muse over the irony of Angela's situation. A dog that was literally thrown away by society goes on to become a movie star. I don't think Hollywood could have scripted a better ending than that.

CHAPTER 14
Heartaches and Setbacks
■ ■ ■ ■ ■

Photo by Diane Trull

SHAKER

Shaker was a little schnauzer that was picked up by a local animal control. Because he was very sick and skinny, he was placed in their quarantine section. During a visit to a local animal control facility to pick up an unclaimed dog, one of our volunteers noticed how pitiful Shaker looked. She scooped him up, put him in her car, and brought him to DAWGS.

We immediately took him to the veterinarian, where he was diagnosed with diabetes. He was also going blind, probably a result of the diabetes. We were able to treat him and within a few days he was doing much better. After several weeks of treatment, Shaker was ready for adoption.

A young science teacher came to our adoption event and was looking for someone special to be part of his family and to be a classroom companion. As soon as he spotted Shaker, he knew he was the one.

Today, Shaker is in a great family and has found his forever home, as well as an extended family of students.

■ ■ ■ ■ ■

THE YEAR WAS FLYING BY and so were the city council meetings. After sixteen years of service, the current mayor retired in 2005 and Dalhart elected his replacement. We weren't sure what impact, if any, the newly-elected mayor would have on our efforts, but we were hopeful that he would be an ally.

The city council's September meeting rolled around, and once again, the topic of DAWGS was on the agenda. This time the status of our shelter was up for discussion. The city was contemplating taking back the land they had loaned us more than two years ago. Cindy, Katie, and Kat called everybody they knew—from veterinarians to neighbors to friends and family—and asked them to attend the meeting. We wanted a full army of supporters as we defended our position, our shelter, and possibly our future.

"The shelter started out on a small scale," the city manager began. "When DAWGS first started, you had probably twenty dogs. Today, with almost five hundred dogs, the barking has become bothersome. We didn't anticipate it, and I'm sure you didn't either. At certain times of the day, particularly during feedings, all the dogs seem to be barking at once. It's a nuisance to the residents throughout the neighborhoods and it's very disruptive during funerals and when people are visiting graves at the cemetery."

I could feel my frustration creeping back. As far as I knew, nobody had ever complained about funerals being disrupted by the gunfire from the shooting range before it relocated or the excessive noise from the rumbling freight trains that constantly rolled by. But somehow, the barking that was coming from our shelter was unacceptable.

"I've attended funeral services at the cemetery, and, on occasion, I have heard neighborhood

176

dogs barking," I said. "Typically, our dogs will bark if a garbage truck is removing our garbage, or if the animal control officer is dropping off a new dog, or possibly if a dog has gotten loose on the property while being moved. Regardless of the reason, I agree that it is a problem. We've tried a few things to address it. We've moved our feeding time to late afternoons, and we've asked the animal control officer to avoid coming to the shelter to drop off any dogs during a funeral service and also to advise us of the times of any services so we can lock down the shelter. Although these changes have reduced the barking, it's still an issue. We will continue to explore other options as well, but it's not something that we can completely get rid of."

The mayor, however, was not appeased. "Well, the real problem is that your current location is not suitable for the number of dogs in your care. You've completely outgrown the space and, as a result, the noise has become a major issue."

"We're teaching children that they can make a difference," I replied, "and it seems as if you're telling us that what we're doing doesn't matter. Earlier this year, the Wisconsin Educational Communications Board came to visit our shelter. Through their affiliation with Wisconsin Public Television, they produced a television series called 'Democracy It Is!' Each episode depicts students expressing their rights and fulfilling their responsibilities as citizens of their classrooms, schools, communities, states, and nation. Our kids were filmed for a segment called 'Responsibilities of Citizens,' which focuses on taking responsibility for yourself and the world around you.

"Most everybody says they like what we're teaching our children except for some people here in Dalhart. I'm determined to preserve the touching friendships that have developed between these dogs that are starved for love and the children who are eager to give it."

The city manager jumped into the fray. "Diane, we fully recognize and appreciate what a great service DAWGS has been to Dalhart," he said. "You accommodate our strays—as well as dogs that are now showing up from other nearby areas—and you go to unbelievable lengths to get them adopted. It's obvious that the dogs are well cared for and loved. It's just that things have gotten somewhat out of hand as far as the numbers are concerned.

"This council has a responsibility to all of the residents of Dalhart, and since there are ongoing complaints about the noise, it's not something we can ignore. We have to address the problem and find a solution."

The mayor looked at us solemnly. "Diane and Mark, I'm sorry to be the bearer of bad news, but, after much deliberation, it has been decided that we can't allow you to stay on the city's property any longer. You will have to find a new location to house all of your hounds, preferably some place that is more suitable for the overwhelming number of animals in your care. And if you're not successful in finding a new location, then we'll be forced to shut down the shelter. We do recognize, however, that with winter starting in a few months, the weather may affect your ability to move in a timely manner. We will try to be as flexible and accommodating as we can with the actual deadline."

Mark and I were dumbfounded. Despite all of their supportive talk, it appeared the city had been against us from the start. The fact that we were saving hundreds of lives and teaching children core values of compassion and empathy for others was, at the end of the day, not enough. But even with our differences, we never expected that the city would go as far as to threaten to shut us down. We were feeling so defeated but knew we had to go on... for the animals and for the children.

Two weeks later, on October 4, 2005, we officially received the bad news, compliments of a certified letter. The city was taking back their land. The letter stated that a local company wanted to run a connecting rail spur between the two existing railroad lines. The original placement of the spur wasn't near the shelter, but when a farmer complained that the proposed spur encroached on his property, the city opted to relocate the spur. The new design placed the spur within a few feet of the shelter, so the city needed the two acres for the required easement.

I was deeply hurt by this latest turn of events. It appeared the rumors we kept hearing about the proposed spur were true, after all.

The letter ended with a directive: DAWGS must vacate the property by March 1, 2006, or the shelter would be shut down. They were giving us less than six months to find a new place and relocate. I'm usually overly anxious for spring to arrive, but I had a bad feeling that this forced move was going to take the spring right out of my step. My eyes welled up. It was hard to wrap my brain around what the next several months would hold for us.

After the news about our eviction made its way around Dalhart, we were hoping somebody from the area would step up and say, "Hey, I've got a piece of property over here that I'm not using." Ironically, we were offered several locations outside of Texas, some as far away as California, but we couldn't consider those options. Leaving town wouldn't solve Dalhart's unwanted dog problem. And it was the children's shelter.

Mark and I spent an untold number of hours looking at properties, trying to find something that was close enough to town so the kids could continue their mission of caring for the animals they love and enable us to build a proper sanctuary. Our dream was to have both indoor facilities and outdoor areas where the dogs could have plenty of room to run. Even though Texas is known for its wide-open spaces, we were in big-farm country, which meant we weren't having much luck finding a small, reasonably priced parcel.

Adding to our stress of trying to purchase land in a timely manner was another sort of guillotine hanging over our heads, except instead of a blade, the weapon of choice was a needle. The city council members were already hedging their bet that we wouldn't be able to successfully relocate and had put out bids to veterinary clinics in the area to euthanize the dogs. Consequently, they had accepted one of the bids and had budgeted ten thousand dollars to euthanize all of our dogs starting March 1. It was gut-wrenching to hear such horrific plans made so far in advance. I was more determined than ever to be off their property in time.

In the midst of our search for land, there was a sudden flurry of national-media interest in our little sanctuary. Mona, one of our concerned supporters from Pennsylvania, contacted the editors at New York-based *People* magazine and told them about the issues we were facing. *People* has a history of running animal-related stories, especially if the animals are in need of help and protection. The magazine sent freelance journalist Chad Love to Dalhart to write a feature article about DAWGS.

I wasn't sure what to expect from Chad's visit. I welcomed the opportunity to get our story on a larger stage, but the last thing I wanted was to stir up even more controversy with the city. When he arrived, I shared my concerns with him about the story. He assured me the focus of his piece was going to be on DAWGS's mission and accomplishments, and the students.

Chad was extremely thorough in his research. He spent hours at the shelter visiting with the kids and witnessing firsthand the variety of work they do on a daily basis. And when an unexpected thunderstorm dropped the temperatures from the mid-fifties to near freezing one afternoon, everybody went into overdrive. While the kids were busy getting all the animals fed, Chad took off his journalist hat and helped me pitch hay into all the kennels to absorb the excess water that was accumulating as a result of the storm.

The next day, he interviewed several of the families that had adopted dogs from us over the years, as well as the veterinarians who care for our animals. He also spoke to our school's officials and some of the parents of our student volunteers.

But it wasn't until a reporter from the local

newspaper informed Chad about the issues between the city and the sanctuary that Chad changed his focus.

"I believe the ongoing conflict between DAWGS and the city is the real story here, and it needs to be exposed," he told me the day before he left Dalhart. "This is Journalism 101 and I'm not walking away from it."

Shortly after Chad's visit, we were contacted by several other major media sources, including "At Large with Geraldo Rivera" from Fox News and the "Today" show from NBC. "Good Morning America" from ABC also reached out to us regarding an exclusive interview but because we had already talked with the other two shows, we weren't able to grant their request. During the taping of the interviews, we kept our fingers crossed that all the media attention would generate some positive momentum for the shelter, mainly in helping us find some property.

Chad's article "Can These Dogs Be Saved?" appeared in *People* in its December 19, 2005 issue. It was a well written piece that deftly brought to light the differences between the city and DAWGS without any finger pointing. The two national news programs also aired our story that same week. It was a trifecta among the media moguls.

Although I had received an advanced copy of the article before it hit the newsstands, I wanted to have additional copies on hand for the students. Once I knew the magazine was out, I drove to several stores in town hoping to purchase extra copies, only to discover that every store had already sold out. It wasn't until I went to our local grocery store that I learned from the store manager that members of the city council had come through and cleaned out all the racks.

Mark and I were wondering what the city officials thought of all this coverage. Their attempt to silence the story told us all that we needed to know.

A few days later we ran into the mayor at the hardware store.

"So, I'm assuming you saw the article in *People*?" Mark asked.

"I did," he said. His face was expressionless. "Overall, I think the reporter was fair, but I do think the story is getting overexposed."

"Well, we had no control over how the piece was written," Mark said. "Chad wrote the story based on his research and conversations and what he believes to be true."

"I'm sure that's the case, but I certainly hope things start to settle down a bit now."

"Trust me, so do we," Mark said. Then we parted ways.

Unexpectedly, but probably because of the barrage of media exposure, the city voluntarily extended our eviction deadline by two months,

184

moving it from March 2006 to May 2006. The mayor went on record to say that the city would be willing to extend the deadline even longer if we could assure him that we would reduce the shelter population to only thirty or forty dogs.

But there was no way we could do that, especially in such a short time frame. Once again we reminded him (and anybody else who would listen) that we don't determine the number of animals that come into our care. Until the residents in Dalhart and the surrounding communities became responsible pet owners, the numbers wouldn't drop. The homeless animals in our shelter are the tragic consequence of irresponsible people who failed to spay or neuter their pets.

The new year began with a heavy snowfall and a flurry of inquiries from organizations, as well as individuals, across the country that had learned about our sanctuary. Word was definitely spreading, and many kindhearted individuals were eager to offer assistance.

An animal rescue group in Denver, Colorado, donated fifty blankets to help keep our mama dogs and puppies warm during the long winter months. Audit Dog, founded by Milton and Teresa, in San Francisco, California, sent us forty-four thousand pounds of dog food. John Kane with Rescue Bank in Houston, Texas, e-mailed me and said they had two loads of dry dog food ready to ship to us. (Rescue Bank is a nonprofit pet-food pantry that applies the human food-bank model by providing donated food to animal rescue groups throughout the country.) Each gift was a wonderful reminder of how amazing and generous people can be.

The requests for interviews from multiple major media sources also kept pouring in, as well as continuing coverage from our local television stations and newspaper. Animal Planet and PBS were just two of several television outlets that expressed interest in our story. It seemed that the animal version of David and Goliath was just too tempting to pass up.

But as more and more interview requests came in, Mark and I realized that, in the long run, all this attention wasn't helping our situation. We did not want to continue perpetuating our controversy with the city, but the media hounds seemed eager to focus on our differences, perceived or otherwise.

We decided to decline all future requests for interviews, unless a group was interested in hearing about what we were trying to promote. The message that we wanted to spread was our desire to create spay-and-neuter clinics in partnership with the city. Starting such programs, and holding pet owners responsible for their dogs, was what we needed to impact the stray dog problem in Dalhart. In fact, we believed it was the only thing that would dramatically make a difference.

And we desperately needed to get moved.

CHAPTER 15
The Art of Letting Go
■ ■ ■ ■ ■

Photo © 2019 Karen Kuehn

BEN AND JERRY

The animal control agent dropped off two beautiful collie mixes that were local strays. The dogs were often seen sitting by the side of the road waiting for the school bus to go by. The children named the dogs Ben and Jerry after the famous ice cream company and because they wanted two names that would always go together. We quickly learned just how appropriate these names would be.

The first night, we put the dogs in separate pens next to each other, as this provided the most space for them. The next morning, there was a huge hole in the fence where the dogs had chewed through to reach each other. Realizing our error, we put them in a pen together.

The next morning, we found Ben and Jerry had climbed over the fence and were sitting outside the shelter, enjoying their freedom and the sun. We quickly improvised a top on their run so they couldn't escape again.

Over the years, we spent a lot of time working with both dogs and although they became friendlier to people, Ben and Jerry did not like to be separated. Many people expressed interest in them, but no one wanted to adopt them together. After three years of living at the sanctuary, a couple who recently had lost their two beloved Pyrenees came to see our dogs and they fell in love with Ben and Jerry.

When we did a follow-up visit on the dogs, we learned that the only complaint the family had about Ben and Jerry was that they hog the bed!

■ ■ ■ ■ ■

THE DOGS THAT GOT TURNED OVER to our shelter arrived in varying degrees of health, confidence, and temperament. Some had never felt loved. Others had had a hard life of nonstop breeding. A few lucky ones may have come from good homes, but because of financial difficulty or changes in family status, they had to be relinquished. Their backgrounds were as varied as their breeds.

Whenever we got a new arrival that required special attention and care, we instinctively turned to Jesse. Even though most of us lovingly called him "Johnny-on-the-spot" because of his eagerness and devotion to help these delicate souls, Mark gave him the honorary title of "TLC Coordinator," or in other words, the Tender Loving Care Coordinator.

And that's how Jesse became attached to Feeney, a yellow shepherd mix that was left on our doorstep. She arrived with a host of medical issues, but mainly what she needed was love.

"Can I be Feeney's main caretaker?" Jesse asked a few days after we got her settled in. "I think if she sees me every day and gets used to having me around, she'll start to be less afraid."

"I think you're the perfect person to help bring her out of her shell," I said. And I did think that. As my students grew older, their intuition about how to care for the dogs was also evolving.

Jesse's knack was helping dogs with trust issues.

Jesse took his role with Feeney seriously, and it didn't take long for the two to become fast friends. As their friendship and trust developed, Feeney's sweet personality blossomed.

Then the unthinkable happened.

A young family came to the sanctuary one day and fell in love with Feeney. And just like that, she was whisked away to her new home.

Jesse was heartbroken.

Although we knew in our minds that adoption is always the goal, our hearts always broke a little when the dogs had to leave us. And for whatever reason, some animals created a bigger void than others. For Jesse, Feeney was that dog.

Jesse struggled for a long time after Feeney left. Weeks after the adoption, I was concerned Jesse was still upset.

"Would you like a ride home, Jesse?" I asked him one night when we were finishing up our rounds at the shelter.

Jesse and Alicia lived with their grandmother a few miles away from the sanctuary. I often gave them a ride home to save their grandmother from making a trip to the shelter, especially after dark. Plus, I wanted a chance to talk with Jesse, and I thought giving him a ride might be the perfect opportunity.

"So, are you okay?" I asked after we had been on the road for a few minutes. "I've noticed that you've been a little quiet lately. Is it because you still miss Feeney?"

"Yeah, I guess so," he said, peering out the window.

Although it was pitch-black outside, I knew he was seeing Feeney's face in the darkness.

"I mean, I'm glad that she got adopted and all, but I keep thinking about her new family. I wonder if they're going to treat her well and play with her. Will they give her a good home and protect her like I did? Are they going to feed her and give her fresh water every day? It's really hard for me not to think about all that whenever any of our dogs get adopted, not just Feeney."

"Well, those are all genuine concerns, Jesse," I assured him, "and I think it's only natural to have those thoughts since we spend so much time with all of our rescues. But we have to remember that there are a lot of people who really love their pets, and although they may not do things exactly the same way we might, they will do the right thing in caring for them. Plus, dogs are very resilient, and they can usually adapt to new situations a lot easier than most people.

"But I know you've been worried about Feeney, so yesterday I called her new owners to see how things were going. The woman assured me that Feeney has settled in nicely and that she's already a big part of their family. Hopefully that will make you feel a little better, knowing that she's safe, happy, and loved."

He glanced over at me and a small smile touched his lips. "Thank you, Mrs. Trull. It does."

THE FOLLOWING MONTH fate stepped in and brought us another exceptionally needy dog. We found the timid shepherd mix tied to the shelter's front gate during a blinding snowstorm, and Mark felt that the dog needed Jesse's special touch after her traumatic arrival.

"Okay, Jesse, I think you've got your next project," Mark said. "And I think we should name her Fawney."

It didn't take long for Mark's intuition to be proven right.

Like Feeney, Fawney was shy and skittish. And, like Feeney, Fawney learned to trust Jesse, and the two bonded over time. Whenever Jesse disappeared, we knew that we would find him in Fawney's kennel.

"I really wish I could adopt Fawney as my own dog, Mrs. Trull," Jesse confided in me one Saturday afternoon. We were making the rounds, checking that all the kennel latches were working properly. The last thing we needed was a faulty latch on a kennel to encourage an aspiring escape artist.

"Have you talked to your grandmother about the possibility of adopting her?" I asked.

"I have, but she's afraid that Fawney is too big of a dog for our house," Jesse lamented.

"Well, why don't you ask her if you could bring Fawney home for one night and see how things go," I suggested. "If nothing else, I bet Fawney would enjoy having a break from the shelter."

Jesse could barely contain his excitement when his grandmother agreed to the sleepover.

And because the visit went well, Fawney continued to stay with Jesse night after night.

But, after a few weeks, Jesse's grandmother, who worked hard to keep the household in order, decided that caring for Fawney was too much work. She gently broke the news to Jesse that they wouldn't be able to keep the dog.

And, once again, Jesse's heart was broken. After Fawney was returned to the shelter, Jesse continued to spend whatever free time he had with her until she was adopted.

It was obvious that Jesse was still missing his friend weeks later.

"It's just hard for me not to be thinking about that special dog," he said when I asked how he was doing.

"I know how much you cared for Fawney, and you're right, she is special," I agreed. "But hopefully you recognize your part in helping her overcome her fears so she could find her forever home. That's the best gift you could have given her."

There are a lot of parallels between some of our rescued animals and some of the kids who have participated in our program. They share similarities in that many come from dysfunctional backgrounds, broken families, and unstable homes. The kids come to the shelter, find stability, and get a chance to do something that makes them feel good about themselves. In return, the animals get to experience unconditional love and learn to trust again.

At the end of the day, the kids see the difference they've made in the animals' lives, and that sense of accomplishment directly impacts their own lives.

So many times, people have come to the shelter and expressed their surprise at how friendly and approachable our rescues are. Our dogs are wonderful, and Mark and I have no doubt it's because of the constant interaction between the kids and the animals. The children are the reason for our success. They don't just feed the animals and leave. They walk the dogs, visit with them, and get close to them. They know each of them in their own way and shower them with love. I believe that's the "X factor" in what makes our shelter different from all the others.

CHAPTER 16
A Most Unlikely Reunion

■ ■ ■ ■ ■

STEWIE

Savannah had received a piggy bank for her birthday and was saving money to adopt a dog from DAWGS. After several months, she had enough money saved and she and her mother came to the shelter to adopt. Savannah carefully looked at all the dogs and puppies, trying to find that special one. But fate stepped in when she walked by Stewie's cage.

Although Stewie was hiding under his blanket, when he heard Savannah's voice, he jumped up and gently grabbed her fingers. It was love at first sight.

He was a pitiful little Tuxedo cat that was heard crying insistently after a storm. We were contacted by a concerned elderly woman and went to look for the cat. We finally found him, wet and shivering on a doorstep. We knocked on the door to see if the cat belonged there. The homeowner answered the door and stated the kitten was not hers and that she was keeping her TV turned up as loud as possible so she wouldn't have to hear the kitten crying.

Once we fed him, Stewie snuggled into the blanket we had carefully put into his crate, and his cries instantly subsided. He was a very content cat.

Although Savannah originally had her heart set on adopting a dog, after holding Stewie her plans changed.

Today, Savannah and Stewie are the best of friends who spend hours playing dolls and snuggling together on cold nights.

■ ■ ■ ■ ■

I T'S TAKEN ME A LONG TIME to summon up my strength to come here," the woman softly announced as she walked in. "Emotionally, that is. Not physically."

Molly and I had been folding an assortment of towels and bedding fresh from the dryer, but we put our chores aside when the woman arrived. She was bundled in a heavy coat, and there was an air of sadness around her tall, slender figure.

I wasn't sure what she meant, but I welcomed her to the shelter and waited to hear what she had to say. Everybody has a story, but not everybody is willing to share it.

We learned that our visitor's name was Linda and that she was a long-time resident of Dalhart. We also learned that she was still reeling from the loss of her canine companion.

"I lost my beloved black Labrador exactly a year ago today," Linda began. "Dottie was my constant companion and loyal friend. She was everything to me and I was heartbroken when she died."

Linda explained that Dottie had somehow escaped from her fenced-in backyard one afternoon. When she realized that Dottie was gone, she immediately contacted Dalhart Animal Control to report her dog missing. Linda was devastated when she got a return phone call telling her that Dottie had been found dead on the side of the road. A hit-and-run.

"I've been grieving for an entire year," Linda admitted. "And although I will always miss my special girl, I realize it's time for me to help another dog, and hopefully find a new best friend in the process."

"Well, we've got some really great dogs here," Molly assured her. "Mrs. Trull, will it be okay if Jesse and I walk around with you two as you look at all the dogs? We can tell Ms. Linda a lot about each one and that might help her decide on which one to get."

After we threw on our jackets, our eager escorts led us toward the first row of kennels. And Molly was right. Because the kids spend so much time at the shelter, they are great ambassadors for all our dogs. They know the temperaments and quirks of each one, which dogs are good around kids, which ones need a lot of physical activity, and which ones are great lap dogs. All this information helps potential adopters find their perfect match.

"We really need to take our time visiting every dog," Molly said. "Some of them can be a little shy at first, but they have just as much love to give as the others. The best thing to do is to let the dog pick you."

"What type of dog do you think you want?" Jesse gently probed. I think he sensed the fragility of Linda's emotions, and he didn't want to upset her further.

"Truthfully, I really don't know," Linda replied. "I didn't want to come here with my heart set on getting a certain breed or a certain colored dog only to be disappointed if I couldn't find what I was looking for. What's most important is that I find a dog that makes me feel the way Dottie did. I really miss not having a dog in my life."

As we meandered through the sanctuary looking at all the dogs, we could hear urgent whining and barking coming from one of the dogs several rows away. The animal was clearly agitated.

"Who's making all that noise?" Jesse semi-whispered to me.

"I don't know, but whoever it is they sound really unhappy," I whispered back. "Go and see if you can calm down whoever it is before we make our way over there."

When Molly, Linda, and I caught up to Jesse, we saw him squatting inside one of the pens trying to soothe an adult black Labrador retriever named Hope. Normally a calm and reserved dog, she was whimpering and crying while frantically pacing back and forth along the front of her chain-link kennel.

"I don't know why she's so upset," Jesse said, looking up at us almost apologetically.

Linda stopped in her tracks. "Dottie?!" she cried out. "That's my Dottie! But how can that be? What is she doing here?"

We stood dumbstruck while Linda ran to the dog, tears streaming down her face. Hope started jumping all over her as soon as she entered the kennel. The dog Linda had lost more than a year ago was alive and well in front of her.

It took several minutes for Hope to calm down enough for us to sort out the mysterious chain of events. Only then did we realize how close this reunion of a lifetime almost came to never happening.

Hope's name, as it turns out, couldn't have been more appropriate.

As best we could recount, Dalhart Animal Control had found Linda's dog roaming the streets and took her to their facility. Somehow, they confused Linda's dog with another dog they had found that same day that had been killed by a car. Around the time that Linda was trying to find her lost dog, I pulled the pretty lab from the city pound when her allotted time was up. Upon her arrival at the shelter, the students agreed that her name should be Hope.

"When I got the phone call telling me that Dottie was dead, I accepted the news at face value," Linda said, still shaking her head in disbelief. "It never occurred to me that there could have been some sort of mix-up or that somebody else might have rescued her. And all this time she's been right here, practically in my own backyard."

"I'm so happy you found your dog," Molly said. "We've loved her and have taken good care of her just as if she were our own pet." She leaned over and kissed Dottie on her silky head.

"I can see that," Linda said. "And it's definitely a comfort to know she wasn't mistreated or suffering in any way. I can't thank you enough for all that you've done in caring for her. I still can't believe I have my precious girl back."

Linda gave each of us a big hug and took the dog's leash from Jesse's outstretched hand. Dottie was still jumping around, excited to be reunited with her owner.

"Wow, that was pretty cool," Jesse said as we watched Linda and Dottie drive off together.

The only thing missing for a perfect Hollywood ending was a beautiful sunset.

"Yeah, things don't get much better than that," Molly agreed.

It was definitely one of those moments that reminded us why we work so hard for the animals in our care. The one thing we want more than anything is for our dogs to go to good homes. And although it's rare to be part of a homecoming story with such unbelievable odds, this is just one of the many reasons why we rescue.

CHAPTER 17

Growing Pains

■ ■ ■ ■ ■

Photo by Diane Trull

TANNER

We received a call from an Amarillo veterinary clinic regarding a Labrador retriever mix that had been brought in to be euthanized. Apparently, Tanner had had a seizure and his family decided they didn't want him with his illness. We took Tanner to a foster home, where he thrived on medication prescribed by the veterinarian.

Month after month, we took Tanner to our weekend adoption events, but no one was ready to commit to an animal with seizures. We personally had never witnessed him having a seizure. At a local festival where DAWGS had a booth, a nice young man, who was also named Tanner, stopped by. When he met Tanner, the dog, he decided it was destiny that the two should be together.

Tanner, the man, is a nurse and is well equipped to handle any health issues that might occur.

A few weeks later, we contacted the two Tanners and learned that Tanner, the dog, was doing great, and that Tanner, the man, thinks he has the most amazing dog ever.

■ ■ ■ ■ ■

THE SHRILL OF THE RINGING PHONE woke me with a start. A quick glance at the clock told me it was just after midnight. Seldom does anybody call in the middle of the night with good news. Sitting up in bed, I studied Mark's face as he listened on the phone, searching for any clue as to what the call was about.

"I'm not sure who that was but they claim to have just driven by the shelter," Mark said, hanging up the phone. He got up and started throwing on some blue jeans and a sweatshirt; I rolled out of bed, too. "The caller said there were a lot of dogs running loose outside the fence," he continued. "If that's true, the only way something like that could happen is if somebody tampered with the main gate."

"Do you think it was a prank call?" I asked, putting on several layers while looking longingly at our warm bed. I wondered if we would be getting any more sleep that night.

"No, I don't think so. There was genuine concern in his voice."

I grabbed my cell phone as Mark and I raced out of the house and hopped into his truck. It was an unpleasantly cold January night and the moon was barely visible through the murky clouds. I called Katie and Tyler, as well as Kat and Cindy, and asked them all to meet us at the shelter. I hated waking them up in the middle of the night, but since I didn't know how bad the situation was, I wanted to have as many hands on deck as possible.

It was only a short drive from our house to the sanctuary, but the journey felt endless. I was anxious and uneasy as the bumpy dirt road jostled my thoughts as much as my body. Mark and I were hoping the situation wasn't as bad as it sounded.

Approaching the shelter, we could hear incessant barking before we could see anything. Mark slowed the truck and the beams of the headlights silhouetted a slew of dogs racing around. A handful of dogs were running loose outside the front gate while a larger number were zipping around the open area inside the shelter. All the dogs were barking at the strange vehicles with flashing lights and the people moving around in the dark.

Two police officers and an employee from animal control were already on site when we arrived. Apparently, the same individual who had called us had also called the police. The three officials were doing their best to keep the dogs corralled within the area.

One of the sergeants of the Dalhart Police Department met us as we got out of the truck.

"Sorry about what's happened out here, folks," she said. "It's really unfortunate. We found what's left of the main padlock lying on the ground. Whoever did this used some heavy-duty bolt cutters. Clearly, they were on a mission. We also found an identification card and a glove that was dropped by the front gate. Hopefully, that's enough evidence to give us a solid lead in finding who did this."

I was already overwhelmed, but when I looked past the sergeant, my heart sank even further. As far as we could see, every kennel gate was wide open. Whoever did this was obviously trying to set all the dogs free.

As we worked to get the dogs safely back into their pens, my mind tried to make sense of what had happened. Why would somebody purposely do this, and what were they hoping to accomplish? Were the trespassers a bunch of kids just playing a practical joke, or was it somebody more sinister trying to send us some sort of message? We already knew that some of the neighbors were irritated by the barking, but the kids were providing a meaningful service to the community. It just didn't add up.

Luckily, the majority of the dogs chose not to take advantage of their newfound freedom. Although we estimated about sixty dogs running loose inside the shelter, most never ran past the front gate. And those that had, quickly returned when they'd heard all of our trucks pull up. What was even more miraculous was that despite so many opened kennels, most of the dogs had opted to stay inside them.

After the sergeant left, Katie, Mark, and Tyler worked the rest of the night to round up the few remaining loose dogs while Cindy made sure everybody was locked back up in their proper pens and with their proper kennel mates. There were a few dogs that were sporting minor injuries because of some dog fights. Kat and I were able to treat most of them on the spot. Two of the dogs had more serious injuries, which would require a visit to the veterinarian the next morning. Considering what could have happened, we were lucky. And grateful.

"I'm so sorry that we had to drag you out of your warm beds on this chilly night," I said to the group after we had wrapped everything up. "I don't know why we keep having these kinds of issues, but we're always grateful for your help. Hopefully, everybody can go home and catch a few hours of sleep before coming back here later."

"Well, if it's any consolation, Diane, we're just as upset by all of this as you and Mark are," Kat said. "All of you work so hard and make countless personal sacrifices just to help the animals. I wish those folks who don't understand why we do what we do would just leave us alone instead of finding ways to harass us. But through the good, the bad, and the ugly, I'm glad to be part of this group. I never stop being amazed by everybody's capacity to care. And I know everyone's tired so I'll get off my soapbox now, but only so I can give each one of you a big hug before we leave."

Kat was a very passionate woman who would often tell us we were her family. And the feeling was mutual. Although she had had a difficult childhood, Kat worked hard to maintain a positive outlook on life. The shelter provided a safe place for her to heal. After volunteering with us for a few months, she'd announced that she was nicknaming the shelter "The Second Chance Ranch," because we weren't just rehabilitating dogs, we were also rehabilitating people.

"You know what I find really interesting?"

Mark said as we were driving home. It was almost seven in the morning and the soft amber glow of the early morning sunrise was peeking over the horizon. "I would have thought more dogs would have inherently run away given the chance. But the fact that they stayed put for the most part suggests that dogs don't necessarily seek freedom to explore. Or maybe they just realize what a great gig they've got there at the shelter and don't want to leave."

Mark winked at me. I knew he was trying to lighten my mood.

"It boggles my mind that this even happened," I replied, still mulling over the events of the night, trying to make sense of the senseless. "For all the good that we're doing, I guess there will always be some folks who will never appreciate or understand what we're doing. But what's even more upsetting is the extreme lengths they will go to try and stop us. I can't help but feel that this is a malicious personal attack in an attempt to discredit animal rescue as a whole."

"Well, as bad as it was, things could have been worse. A lot worse," Mark said. "This was certainly a wake-up call, both literally and figuratively. We'll need to beef up security around the facility and be more diligent in asking the police to patrol the area regularly. It's something we probably should have done a long time ago."

"If the police are successful in catching who-ever did this, are we going to press charges?" I asked.

"I don't know. I certainly don't want to con-tinue stirring up things with members of the community, but at the same time, I don't want to give the impression that we're an easy target. Let's see what they uncover and then we'll decide what to do. Hopefully, all of this will be resolved quickly."

The identification card that the police found on our property belonged to a local high school student. We had no way of knowing if this young man acted alone or if others were involved with the break-in. Despite Mark's repeated inquiries to the police department about any progress being made on the case, no one was ever apprehended or even brought in for questioning.

When Mark specifically asked about checking the identification badge for fingerprints, he was told that the department didn't have the capability to do that. Although we continued to press the police to do something, they never gave us a solid reason as to why the case was quietly dropped.

For the longest time, I felt a little on edge wondering if this young man would continue with his pranks.

CHAPTER 18

A Race Against Time

■ ■ ■ ■ ■

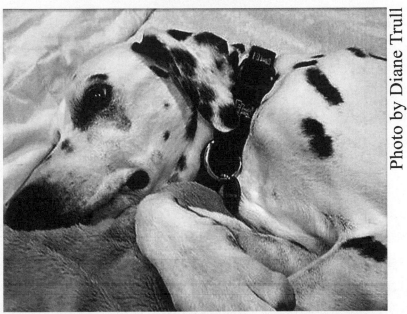

Photo by Diane Trull

BULLET

Bullet was an eight-year-old dalmatian. He was a member of an Amarillo family for his entire life when tragedy struck. There were massive wildfires in the Texas Panhandle, and Bullet's family home was destroyed. His owners were unable to keep him and surrendered him to us. The family asked us to hang on to Bullet, promising to come back for him soon.

We waited a year, but his owners never called

or came back for him. As Bullet sadly waited for his family to return, we got to work on finding him another home.

He is now in a wonderful family where he is very loved and incredibly spoiled!

■ ■ ■ ■ ■

ON APRIL 18, 2006, THE CITY COUNCIL called a special council meeting. Apparently, they were tired of our inability to find a solution to our situation, so they felt it was in their best interest to speed things up.

The meeting began with several council members introducing a motion that would revoke the former resolution in which the city pound was made a no-kill facility. Reversing the pound's status would allow the city to broaden its definition of which dogs they could euthanize.

The former resolution, which had passed three years earlier, also cited that DAWGS was not obligated to accept any animal from the city pound that was deemed vicious or injured to the point that they could not be saved. If those unfortunate animals weren't claimed within seventy-two hours, the city had the right to put them down.

However, since our eviction notice, the city was constantly pressuring us to get our numbers down. They had stopped releasing all their unclaimed dogs to us and started euthanizing the healthy ones because they felt we weren't in a position to accept any new dogs. It was a stressful and heartbreaking situation.

"Our numbers are improving," Mark said. "Cindy, one of our consummate volunteers, is originally from Colorado. Through her connections with different animal rescue groups in that area, we've been able to develop relationships and move some of our dogs out there on a regular basis. We have more room at the shelter now than we did a few weeks ago."

"Well, that may be true," the police chief said, "but we need clarification on what to do with these animals in the interim. The city doesn't have the capacity to hold all the unclaimed dogs, and the backup kennels at the police department aren't big enough to accommodate them either."

The mayor jumped in and said, "Well, I think that's why we have to say that we are officially euthanizing dogs now. If we don't, then we are going against what a previous city council decided when they voted to make the pound a no-kill facility."

"I agree," the city manager said. "It's time to start reducing the sanctuary's numbers. You have way too many animals out there right now. We have to help you limit the number of animals in your care. We should only be releasing the dogs that are highly adoptable. I think the public is getting tired of all of this."

"But the question becomes how do we decide which ones are adoptable," the mayor said.

"Our animal control officer can make that decision," the city manager replied. "We trust his judgment. He's been in his position long enough to know most of the owners and their dogs and where they belong. Plus, it's pretty easy to tell if a dog looks like he's being fed and taken care of and might have accidentally gotten loose versus a dog that's been on his own and eating out of dumpsters for months."

"I think the definition of *adoptable* is debatable," Mark interjected. "It depends on a lot of factors. You can't just look at a dog and say if it's adoptable or not. We've had several dogs that were at our shelter for a couple of years and we had fully expected them to live out the rest of their lives with us because they had been overlooked at numerous adoption events, but when we shipped them off to Colorado, they were adopted immediately. For whatever reason, that area of the country has a different perspective on what's adoptable.

"All we're asking is that we remain involved in the decision-making process. We still want the right of first refusal. If we decline to accept an animal because we don't have room for it, then yes, the city has the right to euthanize it. But I don't see the need to change what's already in place. It's been working fine these past few years."

Despite Mark's comments, the city attorney advised passing a resolution that would reverse the city's no-kill status.

"Before you take a vote," I said, "I'd like to reiterate that changing the city's no-kill policy might create serious trouble for us as we seek financial help in relocating our facility."

"Well, since you've brought it up," the mayor said, "can you give us an update on the status of the properties you're looking at?"

"We've made offers on three potential sites," I replied, "and two fell apart because there were people from within the community telling the property owners not to sell to us because of our plans to build an animal sanctuary. We're still waiting to hear back on our third offer. We've also applied for several grants to help cover the construction costs of some of the buildings, but we must have the land in place before they will talk to us. So, in short, nothing has worked out so far. But, as soon as we close on some land, we'll start meeting with fencing companies and contractors and we'll make arrangements to get the utilities set up."

"As we told you before, we have the backing of a foundation located in Amarillo," Mark said. "However, their philosophy is based on a shelter and city working together to solve animal control problems. A perceived rift between Dalhart and DAWGS could jeopardize our relationship with them, which in turn would jeopardize the future of our shelter. We are on the verge of developing a facility that will help Dalhart's homeless dog problem. We are very, very close to making this a reality. What benefit would it be to rescind the no-kill status now?

"The mayor and I have had many conversations and I think philosophically we understand each other. We all want to reduce the dog population in our town as quickly as possible. That's why Diane and I work as hard as we do trying to find new ways to solve this overwhelming problem. It's in everyone's best interest to get this project going in a direction that works for everybody."

"I guess I don't understand why you're so against euthanasia as an option for getting a handle on things," the city manager said. "Sterilizing a dog or euthanizing a dog, the net result is that you eliminate more dogs. And euthanasia would help get your numbers down."

"I'm sorry?" I stuttered, not believing what I had just heard. "I think I misheard you. Would you please repeat that?"

But when he repeated his comment, I finally realized just how far apart we were in our thinking. Yes, it cost approximately the same amount of money to euthanize a dog as it did to spay or neuter a dog. But given the option, hands down, I would rather sterilize a dog, feed it, care for it, get it back to health, and then get it adopted into a loving home.

In spite of our passionate pleas, the council members appeared to have already made up their minds when they called for a vote. The motion, which passed unanimously, gave the animal control department authorization to euthanize any homeless dog it received, whatever the reason.

And with that one swift vote, it felt as if everything had come full circle. We had worked so hard to make sure as many animals as possible had a second chance at life. Yet, the city's officials were choosing to revert to their old ways while ignoring the real problem that pet owners weren't taking responsibility for their pets.

It was a bitter pill to swallow.

By the middle of June, Mark and I were negotiating with the owner of a third property on which we had made an offer. Luckily, the third time turned out to be the charm for us, although the deal wasn't without drama.

The property we were interested in was formerly owned by a farmer who had filed for bankruptcy. One of Dalhart's local residents had then taken the property out of bankruptcy and was interested in flipping it as quickly as possible. An incredible woman, Janet, had been watching what was going on with the city. She had seen the Geraldo program, and the situation made her mad. She contacted the property owner, started the negotiations, and made a generous down payment with the help of George and Thomas.

It was at this point that the seller told us he had been contacted by someone associated with the city with a counteroffer. Apparently, that person was interested in raising organic cows and felt this particular site would work best for their plans. After several conversations with the seller—who was tempted to take the city up on their offer—he agreed to honor our original deal.

With the land now in escrow, we needed to raise a considerable amount of money. Due to the city's unwillingness to help with land, the Amarillo foundation that had offered us funding for the new shelter, withdrew their offer. They wanted the project to be a collaboration with the city and without controversy. When the director of the foundation heard about the city's budget for euthanizing the dogs, she told me that maybe they were right; the dogs were only mutts and perhaps we needed to let the city put them down.

Obviously, I disagreed with her.

We were fortunate in that Jerry and his wife, Bertie, two of our most loyal and longest-standing supporters from Houston, graciously provided the balance of funds we needed to purchase the land. (Jerry and Bertie, along with Joey, a donor from New York, had also co-purchased a truck and travel trailer for the shelter in its early years.

When they'd heard we were making weekly trips to Amarillo's adoption events with only a handful of animals because our trailer was too small, they donated a brand-new trailer that accommodated up to thirty animals. That trailer was a game changer!)

Within a few weeks, DAWGS had found its new home, soon to be located in the middle of three hundred and twenty acres on Farris Road. The site was six miles east of town, close enough that the kids wouldn't have to travel far to help with the dogs.

When we notified the city that we had officially purchased some land, they extended our deadline to move off their property to March 1, 2007. In theory, eight months sounded like more than enough time to coordinate a move, but we were starting from the ground up, so there was a lot of work to be done. Developing a site takes time, money, and a bit of luck. And if our track record so far was any indication, I knew the rest of the year would be nothing short of interesting.

We were anxious to start the construction process, but our funds were low. Our biggest priority for the new shelter was to build a secure perimeter fence so the dogs couldn't dig their way out. But the kind of fence we wanted to construct wasn't cheap. Ken and Nancy, two of our regular donors in California, sent us a check for fifty thousand dollars, so we were able to hire a fencing contractor. The fence was going to encompass fifty-eight acres and would be set in a trench twelve inches deep. The trench was excavated, then filled with concrete, after which a ten-foot-high steel fence was set into the concrete. Jeff and Susan covered the cost of the concrete.

When we got the first side of the perimeter fence in place, prisoners from the local jail helped us build the individual pens. We used the perimeter fence as the back wall for each pen. By doing that, we only had to purchase two side panels and a gate panel per kennel, which greatly reduced our costs. But because we were erring on the side of caution, we wanted to reinforce the sides of the pens so the dogs couldn't slip under and get into a neighboring run. We purchased hog panel made from galvanized wire rods and cut it the same length as each side of the runs. We buried the hog panel a foot down into the ground on each side and then wired each side panel to the hog panel. Our dogs weren't going anywhere!

After we finished building one row of pens on the south side of the property, the city intervened and put a stop to the prisoners helping us. Without their assistance, it was going to take a lot longer to construct the rest of the pens. But we were bound and determined to make our shelter as safe as possible, so we trudged on with building the pens one at a time, when we had the time.

In addition to the perimeter fence, we were facing other major expenses. The price tag for bringing in electrical lines was ten thousand dollars. Another fifteen thousand dollars was needed for the installation of the water well. Ellen answered our plea for paying for the electrical lines and building a small steel building. Nancy, Barb and John paid for the water well. Leslie, Karen, Rose, Bill, and Alice purchased four hundred new kennels. We were so blessed.

Unfortunately, Mother Nature also wreaked havoc on our plans. Over the next few months, Dalhart experienced every weather condition imaginable—thunderstorms, sleet, hail, three snowstorms, and a tornado that set down thirteen miles from our new location. The weathermen were in their meteorological element. We couldn't get the roadway poured due to flooding in the area, and without a roadway, the contractors responsible for putting in the water well and electrical lines couldn't get to our property.

At the next council meeting, the mayor made it clear he wasn't happy with our slow progress. "We're concerned that in spite of the time you've had to move, it still hasn't happened and that you'll take whatever time we give you, and more, to finish the move. It seems like that's been the case all along."

"You're taking this down an adversarial path, which it doesn't have to go," Mark said. "It's in both of our interests to solve this in a way that's not detrimental to the community, and benefits what we're trying to accomplish. Trust me, there is zero benefit to our staying at the current location."

Regardless of our claims, the city was not happy with our lack of progress.

CHAPTER 19

Rome Wasn't Built in a Day

■ ■ ■ ■ ■

Photo by Diane Trull

SAMMY

Sammy was bought by a nice woman when he was a cute, fluffy poodle. She loved him greatly until she became sick and passed away. Sammy went to live with her son, who placed him on a chain and put him in the backyard where, day after day, he waited to be loved again.

We received a phone call about Sammy and upon our arrival found that he wasn't recognizable as a poodle, or as a dog. He was a mess of matted fur with sticks and burrs stuck in his coat and paws. When we were able to unhook the chain from his embedded collar, Sammy melted into our arms.

Cindy, one of our amazing volunteers who had experience as a groomer, came right over and began to shave off the years of matted fur. As she worked, she continuously talked to Sammy and he would answer with gentle licks to her caring hands. Hours later, Sammy emerged from his four pounds of matted cocoon, which was a third of his body weight.

We took him to one of our adoption events where an elderly lady fell in love with him and adopted him on the spot!

■ ■ ■ ■ ■

MARK CONTINUED HIS EXPLANATION to the committee. "The economic benefit that DAWGS has put back into the community this year is more than three hundred thousand dollars. That's not some number that we arbitrarily came up with either. That figure comes from our audited nine-ninety tax forms that we're required to file as a nonprofit organization. Our new shelter is an investment in the future of DAWGS as well as an investment in solving the homeless animal problem in Dalhart."

Despite having purchased land outside of the city limits, we were still on the council's radar. I imagined that these monthly summonses to come before the council must be similar to how students feel when they are repeatedly called into the principal's office. Even though we knew what to expect, it always put a knot in my stomach.

"Our new facility is going to be very nice and almost every penny that is being spent building it is going back into the community," Mark said. "With the exception of the fencing contractor, we're using local labor and local materials. We buy pet food from local merchants, often clearing out the shelves at all the Dalhart-area stores. We even buy pizza for the kids from the local restaurants after a long day of working at the shelter. We're doing everything we can to make sure Dalhart benefits from our efforts. The water well and electrical lines are going in and we hope to have the perimeter fence completed in about a month. This project is going to be built.

"And when it does get built, one of our goals is to have a clinic that offers sterilization surgeries at reduced rates. Most of the dogs we get come from people who want a dog but aren't responsible pet owners. They don't spay or neuter because they don't feel it's within their discretionary dollars to have their pet altered. Our clinic will be able to address that problem, which will be a huge intervention."

"As we've reiterated time and time again," one of the councilman said, "the concerns of this council relate strictly to your location. We're supportive of what you're doing, but just not out by the cemetery. Several of us are still getting calls from people complaining about the barking. Folks who live in the area have to get up early in the morning to go to work, and when they can't sleep because of hundreds of dogs barking throughout the night, it's a real problem.

"But now that I see some of the progress you're making at your new location, I'm excited. I personally will continue to support your project, even when you're six miles out of town. And I commend you and Diane for the tremendous job you've been doing."

"We're aware that the barking is bothersome, and we've taken steps to address the situation," Mark said. "Although it takes a little longer, we go around each evening and check that all the latches and gates are closed. If one dog gets out, then it is like he's teasing the others, 'I'm out and you're still in there.'

"Once one dog barks then it spreads like wildfire. During funerals or other events, we keep the dogs that tend to bark the most inside. We don't feed or walk any of the animals during those times. We basically shut down until the funeral is over. But I think it's important to understand that it's not easy to develop solutions to such problems.

"A bigger problem that we're facing, however, is that many of our student volunteers feel a lack of support from the council. I'd like to introduce you to one of our most steadfast and loyal volunteers. Jesse is in junior high now, but he has worked at the shelter since day one. Jesse is just one of many kids who faithfully come out every day and give up their time to save animals and to make a difference. They want to know why the city isn't backing them.

"And that's not through our eyes; that's through the eyes of a child. These kids are intuitive. They read the papers, they hear the gossip. I want to be able to tell them the reason.

"Jesse, do you want to come up here and talk to the mayor?"

Jesse stepped forward.

"So, I'm curious, Jesse," the mayor said. "Why do you and your friends think we don't support the project?"

"Simply because you don't agree with what we're doing," Jesse said.

"We support what you're doing, son. As we've said from the very beginning, it's the location of the shelter that's posing the problem."

"Well, we're a no-kill shelter, and the fact that

you want to go back to killing dogs is the reason we don't think you're supporting us," Jesse said.

"I think the council agrees with what the project stands for and how it encourages the involvement of children," the mayor said. "The current location has simply outgrown its size. There are other people in town we represent, and when we constantly get complaints from them that the shelter is too crowded or it's too noisy, we can't ignore that. But I don't think there's anyone on this council who is against your project."

"I think the issue here is about support versus just tolerating our existence," Mark said. "With all due respect, over the past few years, I think it would be disingenuous to say that the council has supported us. There are several members currently on this council who openly support us but then criticize our organization behind closed doors. I believe that for what DAWGS is giving to the community, the council should be more supportive.

"The shelter has survived tremendous challenges because of Diane, the volunteers, and numerous kids like Jesse. I think that's a testament to their perseverance, their compassion, and their commitment to this project. I'm not here to throw stones, but please understand that we've not had the full support of this council throughout our journey."

It was my turn to jump in now. "People didn't

want to sell us any land to be used as an animal shelter," I said. "They told us they were getting pressure from city officials not to sell to us. And at the last two city meetings, the council has been really confrontational. I urge you to play back your own recorded tapes of the meetings and listen to what was said, and more important, to how it was said."

"I'd like to interrupt if I could," another councilman said. "I think what the Trulls are doing is great. I commend them for helping create the no-kill zone. And I also commend all the children and adults who have donated money, time, and thought into doing the humane thing by not killing these animals. I think the city has aided the Trulls and that the Trulls have benefited the community."

"Thank you for your comments," Mark said. "I think it's important that as we continue on this journey, we form a partnership and solve these problems together. If you look at other communities, they receive a huge amount of support from within. There are also many animal rescue organizations that, if you were to do a comparison, you'd see we only have a slice of their operating budgets, yet we are ten times more efficient than they are—and it's because we have people who are committed to what we're doing out there. We're not trying to create animal activists; we're trying to create community activists. People have lost sight of what we're trying to teach these kids; that we want to plant the seeds of change through them. Instead, they are only focusing on the fact that we've got some barking dogs.

"If you believe in something, you fight for it. No matter what you decide this evening, we're moving forward. I hope it's with your support and not just with your tolerance. We represent a solution to Dalhart's animal problem. And when the project is done and the residents look back, they will see what the shelter has done for the community in teaching children responsibility and life skills, saving dogs and keeping them off the street, and reducing the cost of unwanted animals in this town. It's at that point that I think they'll also ask, 'Was this council responsible for solving the problem and helping to get things done, or were their decisions based on personal biases?' "

At the end of the meeting, the council asked us to file a report in thirty days giving them an update on the construction of the new shelter.

"We're not saying you have to be off the property by then," the mayor added. "We're just asking for a progress report. If you run into issues that you can't control, that doesn't mean that we can't extend the time limit. We'd like information and updates along the way. That's all this council has ever asked."

CHAPTER 20
All in a Day's Work
■ ■ ■ ■ ■

Photo by Diane Trull

SPARKLE

Sparkle was an early Christmas present for us. She was left outside the shelter's front gate tied up in a white pillowcase. Next to the pillowcase was a decorated Christmas plate that had kitten food piled on it. You can imagine our surprise when we arrived to see the pillowcase jumping around, with the precious kitten frantically meowing inside. Other than being very upset from the ordeal, Sparkle was unharmed and started purring as soon as she was freed, cuddled, and fed.

She went to our mobile adoptions and was quickly adopted into a great forever home.

■ ■ ■ ■ ■

WORKING FULL-TIME AT SCHOOL and almost full-time at the shelter was taking its toll on me, physically, emotionally, and mentally. Although I've always loved teaching and being around students, I realized that something needed to change. After much soul-searching and endless conversations with Mark, I decided that I would retire from teaching when the 2007 school year ended, and from then on, I would put all my energy into running the shelter. Mark and I already had a lengthy list of long-range plans, and my hope was to start implementing some of them once I was officially down to one job.

We decided to implement the first one on our list—sponsoring a discounted spay-and-neuter clinic—as soon as possible.

The statistics are heartbreaking. Every year, millions of animals end up in shelters where, according to Best Friends Animal Society, an estimated 2,200 dogs and cats are euthanized every day. More disheartening is that ninety percent of these animals are considered adopt-able. But we can't adopt our way out of shelter overpopulation. Adoption addresses the current problem and prevents animals from being killed, but spaying and neutering prevents the problem in the first place. And you only have to spay or neuter an animal once to stop the cycle.

Mark and I believe the best way to reduce our shelter's intake rates is through targeted spay-and-neuter programs. It's the best tool we have right now. Spaying or neutering is the answer for both the health of the animals and the peace of our own consciences. It can eliminate or reduce the incidence of many health problems that can be difficult and expensive to treat. It also helps dogs and cats live longer, healthier lives. In females, spaying eliminates the possibility of uterine or ovarian cancer and greatly reduces the incidence of breast cancer. For males, neutering eliminates testicular cancer and decreases the chance of prostate disease.

There are benefits for the owner as well. Animals that aren't sterilized often exhibit more behavioral and temperamental problems than do those that have been spayed or neutered. Neutering male pets makes them less likely to spray and mark their territory, too.

The problem of pet overpopulation is created and perpetuated one litter at a time. Cats can reproduce at forty-five times the rate of humans, while dogs reproduce at fifteen times the human rate. In seven years, one cat and its kittens can create four hundred and twenty thousand cats. Similarly, in six years, one dog and its puppies can create seventy-five thousand dogs.

Well aware of these staggering statistics, Mark and I moved forward with sponsoring a city-wide spay-and-neuter clinic, even though we didn't have support from the city. Dalhart's local veterinarians agreed to participate in the clinic, but they didn't agree to reduce their costs for performing the surgeries. Thankfully we received two grants, one from the David D. and Nona S. Payne Foundation and one from the Laura Viola Scott Charitable Trust. These wonderful grants allowed us to underwrite the sterilizations.

Since our goal was to target low-income families, we knew we had to make the surgeries affordable. We decided to hold the clinic in February 2007, in hopes of reducing the number of spring litters we would receive. During the designated month, we charged five dollars for cat neuters and fifteen dollars for cat spays. Dogs were neutered for twenty-five dollars and spayed for forty-five.

Pet owners interested in having their pets fixed were instructed to contact one of the veterinarians in town to schedule an appointment. Prepayment was required to guarantee their appointment. On the day of the animal's scheduled surgery, the owners had to provide proof that their pet was current on its rabies shots. If the shots were due or if they didn't have proper documentation, the animal would be vaccinated during the surgery at the owner's expense.

Our first clinic resulted in the sterilization of one hundred twenty-two dogs and cats from our community. Not surprising, there was a remarkable reduction in the number of animals entering our shelter later in the year. In the spring of 2006, we took in twenty-two litters of puppies and five litters of kittens. After the clinic, our spring 2007 intake numbers dropped to ten litters of puppies and two litters of kittens.

Buoyed by the clinic's success, Mark and I were anxious to find additional resources to sponsor future clinics. We've always believed that owners will do the right thing for their pets if given the opportunity. Ideally, we wanted the city's involvement in assisting with the cost of these surgeries. There are many people who are interested in adopting a pet, but they can't afford the cost of the sterilization surgery, even at a reduced rate. The perfect solution would have been if the city shared our vision and stepped in to subsidize the difference.

DURING THE SPRING, the animal control agent came to my classroom one day after lunch. He said he had a very pregnant and very mean mastiff in his truck. He was going to take her to be euthanized. I followed him to the back of his truck and peeked into the large metal crate. The dog was very big, very pregnant, and very unhappy. But there was also a pleading in her soft brown eyes that I felt she just needed another chance. I asked the officer if he would take the dog back to animal control until school was over and then meet us at the shelter with the dog.

As soon as the bell rang at the end of the day, I loaded up several of my students and headed to the sanctuary. We had a large ten-by-ten-foot closet that had a high ceiling and a big heavy door. We used the space for storing pet food and bedding. As soon as we arrived, we cleared out the closet and found a tall gate that we could put across the door opening. The girls also found a large kiddie wading pool and a soft blanket and set up food and water for the dog.

And then we waited and waited for the dog to arrive.

Finally, after it was dark, the agent showed up at the shelter. He had been on a call since he left us earlier in the day and then decided to get a bite to eat. The entire time the mastiff was in the crate in the back of the truck.

Since it was getting late, we were anxious to get the dog settled into her new space. Mark walked over to the truck and was met by a lot of growling. He had the kids gather up several wooden pallets and we made a gauntlet leading from the back of the animal control truck to the closet door. He then had all the kids step back as he carefully opened the cage door. The dog leaped out and ran through the gauntlet, straight into the closet. Tyler was waiting by the door and slid the gate into place once the dog was inside.

At the same time, Mark noticed some movement inside the animal control crate. There, lying on the cold plastic, were three tiny puppies. The poor dog had given birth in the crate as she bounced around all day in the truck bed. Mark gently handed the puppies to me and together we went to the gate. The dog was really upset. Mark calmly talked to her as he gently placed the puppies into the kiddie pool. Her maternal instincts kicked in and she immediately went to take care of her babies. We left her to settle in.

The next morning, she was calmly laying in the pool with her now ten puppies. The girls named her Nala and we quickly found she was all bluster because she was a sweetheart.

Nala was adopted by a family who lived on the edge of Dalhart. Every day, Nala would sit on their front porch and watch the world go by. The family had a three-year-old son who liked to sit with her and play with his toy trucks.

One night, an unexpected blizzard blew in. Nala's family was busy getting all their farm animals settled. They had left their son and Nala snuggled in the warm house and secure in his room; it was too cold and miserable for them to be outside. Somehow, the little boy figured out how to open the kiddie door and went outside looking for everyone. Nala followed behind him.

The boy wandered off about one hundred feet, but the wind and snow covered his tracks. The mother came back to the house to check on them and panicked when she couldn't find them. She rang the big bell by the back door, which brought everyone running to the house. Everybody started frantically calling for the boy. Nala heard the commotion and started barking. The couple ran to where Nala was barking. Nala had dug a hole in the snow and pushed the little boy inside. She then gently sprawled her big body on top of the boy to keep him warm. She was gently licking his face when the family ran up.

The little boy pleaded for them to get Nala off him because he wanted to help his parents with the cows. Nala wouldn't move until the boy's father told Nala it was okay. Apparently, Nala had gone along for the walk with the boy but sensing the danger, she had kept him warm.

CHAPTER 21

Moving On

■ ■ ■ ■ ■

Photo by Diane Trull

NOEL AND PUPPIES

Noel was a beautiful shepherd that had been dumped in the countryside. Pregnant, cold, and alone, she took refuge in a small, dilapidated shell of a barn to protect herself from an early Texas winter cold front. It was in this facility that she gave birth to her babies. Night after night, the sound of coyotes howling could be heard in the area. Unbeknownst to Noel, a farmer lived nearby and had noticed the reoccurring cries of the coyotes.

The weather had changed to freezing rain, and during a break in the storm one evening, the farmer decided to take a ride around his ranch to investigate. From the headlights of his pickup truck, the man saw that a pack of coyotes had surrounded the old barn. He also saw a dog boldly trying to protect her territory, racing in and out of the barn. To his amazement, he saw the dog fall between two of the coyotes and then quickly pull back and sprint back into the barn.

As the coyotes started to follow the dog, the farmer raised his shotgun and fired several shots into the air. The coyotes quickly retreated into the darkness. The farmer checked the young dog for wounds. Aside from several scratches, the dog was unharmed. As the man was petting her, the dog kept leaving and running back into the corner of the barn. The farmer followed her and found what she had fought so hard to protect— nine puppies!

The next day, the farmer brought Noel and her litter to the shelter. The kids named the nine puppies Dancer, Prancer, Donner, Vixen, Dasher, Comet, Cupid, Blitzen, and Rudolph.

Within a few months, we found loving homes for each and every one of them.

■ ■ ■ ■ ■

THE NOTICE OF THE CITY COUNCIL'S special session scheduled for March 6, 2007, appeared on the front page of the Local News section of the *Dalhart Daily Texan*. It was short and sweet with only one item on the agenda: "Consider agreement with DAWGS on city property near the cemetery."

For once, Mark and I were not invited to this special gathering. I doubt we would have gone anyway. We didn't have the emotional fuel to continue defending ourselves. It was falling on deaf ears anyway.

After we missed the March 1 deadline, the city informed us that they were taking legal action to get us off their property. They issued a formal eviction notice, with the added threat that they were turning off the water on the property. We contacted Claire, an animal lover and a lawyer who we had met through Best Friends Animal Society. (Best Friends Animal Society is a national animal welfare organization working to end the killing in America's animal shelters and bring about a time when there are "No More Homeless Pets.") Her new firm was willing to represent us free of charge. In January 2005, *Best Friends* magazine featured an article titled "The No Kill Kids of Texas" written by Claire and her husband, Jim. The heartwarming article featured several of our student volunteers and their dedication to running the shelter. Over the course of several days, our lawyer negotiated a new agreement with the city. The reason for the special meeting was to allow the council to vote on the agreement, which they unanimously passed.

Under the new agreement, we had until eight o'clock in the morning on April 16, 2007, to move all the animals off the property or else the city would shut off the water and charge us one hundred dollars per day rental fee until we were gone. Once the animals were moved, we had until May 1, 2007, to remove all our equipment and belongings. However, the agreement also stated that if we wanted to leave the perimeter fence and the water faucets we had installed, we would not be penalized. I'm not sure what plans they had for repurposing those items, but I found it interesting that they specifically identified them in the agreement.

The next day I got a call from one of the local reporters; he wanted to discuss the terms of the new agreement.

"I appreciate your interest in what happens to our shelter, but we're not discussing this matter anymore," I said. "We've done all we can do to get moved, but with the challenging weather and life in general, it has taken longer than we had anticipated. We think the new agreement is fair and we don't foresee a problem with being moved by April 16.

"But what I am happy to talk to you about— if you're interested—is the positive effect our shelter has had on the city. Since March 2003, we've taken in more than three thousand seven hundred cats and dogs, saving the city of

Dalhart more than thirty thousand dollars, which would have been the cost to euthanize all those animals."

The reporter ignored my response and continued with his original line of questioning. "According to Dalhart's animal control officer, the city is no longer taking its stray animals to your shelter," the reporter said. "In fact, he said they pretty much stopped doing that at the beginning of the year. He also said that the animals in the city's care are available for adoption, but because of the lack of space at the pound, if they aren't reclaimed by their owner or adopted within three days, they are euthanized. What are your thoughts about that?"

"As I've already told you, I have nothing more to say on the matter," I politely replied. "We are trying to stay focused on the positive by continuing to do our part in helping these innocent animals."

THE PROCESS OF moving from the old site to the new one was slow and tedious. We would load a handful of dogs into the travel trailer, which accommodated thirty animals at a time. We would then dismantle the kennels they had been living in, make any necessary repairs to any of the sections, load the metal panels into the beds of our pickup trucks, and drive fifteen minutes to the new shelter. Before we reassembled the pens, the kids cleaned and pressure washed each one, often in freezing rain and snow. Katie, Tucker, and Tyler were responsible for helping them. The older children and a few adult volunteers were responsible for setting up the kennels once they were cleaned. The youngest of the kids were given the task of taking the dogs for walks or cuddling with them in the bales of hay until their pens were ready. We also treated each dog for worms, fleas, and ticks before placing them into their new clean homes, which were stuffed with piles of fresh hay.

Once the thirty dogs were settled, we started the process all over again. Day after day, week after week, this was our routine until April 16, the day we had to be off the property.

As if the move wasn't stressful and time consuming enough, days before our deadline we were asked to participate in a puppy mill rescue. Puppy mills are commercial dog breeding facilities where profit is given priority over the well-being of the dogs. Female dogs are bred at every opportunity with little to no recovery time between litters. Most puppy mills keep animals in cramped and filthy conditions without proper veterinary care or socialization, which causes illness and disease among the animals. Sadly, most people aren't aware that the cute puppy they purchase from the pet store probably comes from one of the estimated ten thousand puppy mills in the country and that the animal may have a host of health problems.

Although we were stretched to the limit with our upcoming move, I couldn't say no when I got a call about a local Chihuahua breeder who had surrendered her one hundred fourteen dogs. We helped transport many of these poor dogs that were living in deplorable conditions to several no-kill shelters in the area. All one hundred fourteen Chihuahuas in an enclosed area is a pretty yappy experience. Within a month they had all been placed in their forever homes.

And if we didn't already have our hands full, Mother Nature dealt us one final round of nasty weather on April 15. Dawn brought light to a dirty gray sky that showered us in a mixture of freezing rain and snow, unusual but not totally unheard of at this time of year. The wet weather mirrored our mood as we realized the herculean task we were facing. Everybody's emotions were running a little high.

"Mrs. Trull, where do you want us to start this morning?" Jesse asked, clapping his gloved hands together for warmth. His cheeks were already red from the cold. "How many more dogs still have to be moved?"

Because we had been working so hard for several weeks, everybody was tired. Bone tired. It was eight in the morning and I was already exhausted just thinking about everything we had to get done that day. I would have sat down and cried if there had been time.

I looked at Jesse and the other children who were eagerly waiting for their instructions, bundled in their warmest winter gear. I felt guilty asking them to spend another day working in these horrible conditions rather than enjoying a day of fun in the snow. But I also knew there was no other place they'd rather be.

"About one hundred and twenty," I replied, hoping that my voice didn't give away my desperation.

"Well, we've worked too hard to stop now," Jesse said. "Come on, guys. Let's get back to it."

I shook my head at their determination as they trudged off. In spite of impossible odds, they were determined to stay the course and finish the job.

On that final morning, the process began as every other day had during the previous month. The children took turns loading dogs into the travel trailer. The fact that everybody was slipping and sliding in the mud and slush didn't seem to faze the kids or the dogs. As soon as the trailer was full, Kat would make the trek to the new shelter ahead of the pickup trucks that were taking the kennels. The kids would unload the dogs and keep them occupied until their new pens were set up.

Because of the extreme weather, several of the

runs were frozen to the ground. Mark borrowed a forklift from a friend and tried to pry the bases of the kennels from the iced topsoil. But since some of the snow had turned to frozen slush, the wheels of the forklift got stuck and he was forced to abandon his plan.

Determined to get the last remaining pens off the property, Mark and two other men resorted to using pickaxes. As they hacked at the frozen earth around the edges of the kennels, some of the younger kids shoveled the broken pieces into a wheelbarrow. All day long, everybody worked without respite.

One of Dalhart's local television stations, KFDA, sent out a news crew midafternoon to film our progress. But after forty-five minutes of following us around, they decided to leave because it was too cold.

At six p.m., we sent the youngest of the children home. It had been a long, cold day and they were exhausted, physically and emotionally. But they were so worried about what would happen to their beloved dogs if they didn't get moved in time. We assured them as best we could that we would save them all.

At ten o'clock when the newscast was airing, there were a handful of us still on the property moving dogs. Hour after hour, we assembled the dog pens using our trucks' headlights for light. Use of the travel trailer to transport the dogs wasn't possible any longer because the inclement weather had completely washed out the main road. We resorted to shuttling the dogs in crates, two by two, in the back of our pickup trucks. The irony that we were doing the same thing that Noah did in loading up his ark wasn't lost on us.

Our biggest concern at this point was that the dogs would become stressed by the unusual late-night activities, but they seemed to sense the urgency and cooperated.

It was nearing midnight when we finally ran out of steam. We were all weary beyond belief and I personally could no longer feel my feet. We made the difficult decision that there was nothing more we could do that night, even though all the dogs had not been moved.

And that's when we noticed the string of head-lights bobbing along the icy road heading toward us.

"Who on earth would be coming to the shelter at this hour, Mom?" Katie asked.

"I'm not really sure," I said hesitantly. My fear was that it might be one of the city's officials stopping by to give us a hard time. A knot formed in the pit of my stomach. Sadly, I wouldn't put it past them.

As it turns out, the caravan belonged to a group of animal lovers who had seen our story on the news and wanted to help. This amazing group of strangers worked alongside us in the bitter cold as we continued setting up the pens. They were determined to help us meet the city's deadline.

After they left, we kept working until three thirty in the mornig, at which time Mark decided that we were done for the night.

"Look, it's really late and we've all been working hard," he said, "but we need to stop and get a few hours of sleep. Kat, would you please take everybody back to the old shelter in the travel trailer and leave it? Let's plan to meet there first thing in the morning and finish moving the rest of the dogs. There are no words to express how much Diane and I appreciate the sacrifices you've made. There's no way we could have done this without all of your help."

I saw the frustration on everyone's faces, but I knew stopping was the right thing to do. Tired, filthy, cold, and smelly, we said good night to each other and caravanned down the road. Although I was exhausted, I wasn't sure if I would be able to sleep knowing we still had a lot to accomplish before the deadline.

Bright and early the next morning, Mark and I headed back to the old shelter, where we were greeted by Kat and a few of our other volunteers. They were all wearing the same clothes we had left them in a few hours before. There were two kennels left standing on the property and no dogs to be seen.

"Good morning, Mark and Diane," Kat said

cheerfully. I noticed she was holding a large can of Red Bull. She looked amazingly perky for somebody who supposedly only got a few hours of sleep the night before.

Mark and I looked around in amazement.

"Do I understand that you've been out here working all night after we left?" Mark asked the group, a hint of accusation in his voice. "I thought we told you to go home."

"Well, we just couldn't do that, Mark," Kat said, challenging his tone. "Every day, we watch Cindy show up at the shelter and give so generously of her time. And countless times we've seen how you and Diane never give up on anybody, no matter the circumstances. Because everybody's sacrifices and dedication mean so much to us, we refused to give up, too. You can be mad at us if you like, but this shelter is too important to too many people, including us. We simply weren't willing to quit."

I gave her a big hug. "We're not mad, Kat," I said. "We're just deeply touched by your actions. Mark and I certainly weren't expecting this, but we thank you from the bottom of our hearts."

Because the group pulled an all-nighter, all the dogs had been moved except two, which were semi-feral. Our plan all along was to move these two dogs last. We were concerned that if they got away from us during the night, we might not be able to catch them. As we were loading them into their crates, the city manager pulled up to the front gate.

Getting out of his car, he looked around the site and saw two muddy acres of open land pitted with deep ruts. Without saying a word, he got back into his car and drove away.

Although everybody was safely moved and settled into their new pens, we didn't have the luxury of stopping for the day. All the dogs had to be fed and given fresh water. Some needed their medication. It was business as usual at our new location. It took us until eleven thirty that night to finish all the day's chores. But it was a great feeling to be moved.

OVER THE NEXT two weeks, we concentrated on moving the physical remains of our belongings from the city's property. To say it was a mess is an understatement. Rusty tools, trash bags, empty food bowls, torn towels, and garden hoses were strewn everywhere. We sorted what we wanted to keep and what we wanted to give away. By the May 1 deadline, the only physical evidence that the shelter had ever existed at this location was a chunk of concrete where the children had imprinted their handprints, written their names, and expressed their love for dogs.

Because of the help of many dedicated animal lovers, more than six hundred dogs and puppies were moved in five weeks during some of

Dalhart's most brutal weather. It was a tremendous endeavor that truly tested our determination and perseverance to provide for the animals entrusted to our care.

"It's so wonderful to be in our new shelter now, away from all the problems in town," Alix said to Mark and me one morning. "The fact that we have fencing, water, electricity, and a small weatherproof barn with an official bathroom is awesome! Everybody is so happy, especially all the animals!"

Although we were still getting things organized and had a lot of work left to do, I had to agree with Alix. We were all thrilled to have a fresh beginning.

PART THREE

If having a soul means being
able to feel love and loyalty and
gratitude, then animals are better
off than a lot of humans.
                    —JAMES HERRIOT

CHAPTER 22

A Cry for Help

■ ■ ■ ■ ■

STEVIE

Stevie came into our care when his family surrendered him during a blizzard. He was going blind and his family no longer wanted him. We were busy trying to keep all the animals warm in preparation for the heavy snows forecasted and asked the family if they would please keep Stevie safe until after the storm, at which time we would take him.

The couple agreed, drove off, and promptly dumped Stevie on the edge of town. Dalhart's animal control officer found the dog about thirty minutes later; Stevie was standing in the middle of the road, confused and shivering. The officer immediately gave us a call, and Stevie spent the next few days being evaluated by a veterinarian. Stevie had suffered some sort of eye trauma that could have been treated when it happened, but sadly, it was too late to do anything now. He was blind in one eye.

One day, a couple came to the shelter looking to adopt a special dog. They spotted Stevie and knew he was the right dog for them, but they wanted to foster him first to make sure he would get along with their other dog, which was older.

Stevie hopped into the couple's truck and headed to Oklahoma. Once he adjusted to his new surroundings and his new canine buddy, his adoption papers were completed.

■ ■ ■ ■ ■

IT WAS EARLY SUMMER when we received an urgent call from an animal rescue group in Odessa, Texas, a town more than three hundred miles away. They needed help. They were completely full and had nowhere to go with twenty dogs that desperately needed a home. Unfortunately, we were completely full as well, but we knew we needed to do something once we heard their gut-wrenching story.

A local breeder in Odessa had more than thirty dogs tied up on heavy chains and living in makeshift pens scattered around his property. The trailer he lived in had no running water and he had no food for the dogs. By the time the Odessa rescue group had heard about the situation, ten of the dogs were missing. They didn't know if the dogs had run away, died, or if the owner had sold them.

The rescue group told us the breeder was an unsavory fellow. He had had several dealings with law enforcement over the years regarding the treatment of his children, who ranged in ages from eight to sixteen. He also had a lengthy rap sheet of drug abuse. But sadly, no one was willing to do anything about the situation with his animals. The local authorities acknowledged the dogs' deplorable conditions, but repeatedly stated that the animals were the man's property and that he could do with them what he wanted.

Unfortunately, this is an all-too-common problem throughout Texas. In spite of several animal abuse laws in place, many Texas counties fail to enforce them.

After Mark and I agreed to take the dogs, we

started planning for our journey south. Karen, an amazing friend and donor, kindly offered to loan us her truck and large horse trailer for transporting the dogs back to Dalhart. Our trip was fraught with road detours and minor truck trouble, causing us to arrive in Odessa much later than we had hoped.

It was too dark to start the rescue operation, so we checked into a motel for the night. The next morning, we awoke to thunder and lightning and torrential rains. After waiting several hours in hopes that the weather would improve, we decided to head to the property.

When we arrived, we were appalled to see the horrible living conditions for animals and humans. The run-down trailer house had several broken windows. Filthy bed sheets improvising as curtains billowed out through the gaping holes. A warped outside closet door lay on the ground, its hinges broken off. The content of the closet revealed the remains of a rusted-out hot water heater that was tilting halfway out of the enclosure. A small concrete step leading to where the door once hung was cracked and crumbling. The front door, which was partly unhinged, was padlocked with a heavy security lock. Mark and I were amused at the irony of someone being concerned about locking the house when most of the windows were missing.

The entire yard was cluttered with debris. Split

bags of garbage were strewn everywhere and pieces of broken glass dotted the ground. The overpowering reek of rotting food mixed with acrid animal waste permeated the air. A strange odor was coming from inside the trailer, which made Mark and me a bit nervous.

In the front yard was a makeshift doghouse with a huge metal chain attached to it. At the end of the chain was an emaciated pit bull looking at us with huge pleading brown eyes. The chain weighed more than the dog. As we walked around the trailer, we saw two more dogs tied up in a similar fashion. One was a brown pit bull male and the other a German shepherd mix. Running around the yard were two little mixed-breed dogs, both scared to death.

At the back of the property we found another huge chain, which had a large female mastiff attached to it and a tag that said Voodoo. This dog was in terrible shape. Instead of wearing a collar, the poor dog had a chain wrapped tightly around her neck, cutting into her skin. She was soaking wet, too, as the chain wasn't long enough to allow her to reach her doghouse. Next to her was the skinniest dog I had ever seen—another little pit bull mix with five puppies. Because there was no shelter for her or her babies, the momma dog had dug a hole for her puppies and laid over it to protect her babies from the rain.

Behind the trailer were four makeshift pens

made of old wooden pallets standing on end. The pens were littered with animal waste more than a foot deep. Several puppies, only three or four months old, were inside the pens, as well as a small basset hound. They were all standing on top of collapsed cardboard boxes, which probably had once served as their doghouses. They were all whimpering pitifully. A small gray cat slithered around the corner and disappeared under the trailer.

For a few minutes Mark and I were at a loss for words as we tried to comprehend the severity of the scene in front of us. We were unprepared for what we had found. Then we got busy.

With the rain pouring down, we began moving the dogs into the shelter of the trailer. We started with the momma pit bull mix and her babies and then moved all the other puppies. Those that could cohabitate shared an area inside the trailer. When we got to the large mastiff, we discovered that the chain was embedded into her neck one-half inch deep, making the surrounding skin look more like raw hamburger meat. We hadn't brought bolt cutters with us so we had no way to remove the chain. We tried to pull the chain out of her neck, but the weight of the links was too much. As a last resort, we led the mastiff, her chain, the cinder block, and the metal pole, which were all connected, into the trailer. After everyone was loaded up, we fed them and gave them soft blankets to lie on. Then we headed home.

After eight hours, we arrived back in Dalhart and began moving the dogs into their new homes. The kids had prepared everything ahead of our arrival so every kennel was loaded with food, water, some toys, and a Dogloo. (Dogloos are patented outdoor doghouses that help protect animals from the elements. The classic igloo shape of the Dogloo is made with structural foam that keeps the dogs warm in the winter and cool in the summer. It also provides great protection when the dogs want to escape from the sun.)

Our first priority was to free the mastiff, which we had named Voodoo based on her tag, from her literal ball and chain. After several attempts, Mark was able to cut the embedded chain from Voodoo's neck using heavyweight bolt cutters. We gingerly unwound the chain and cleaned the infected area. It would take some time before the skin around her neck would look normal again. With the weight of the chain gone, Voodoo happily shook her head, enjoying her new freedom. We led her into her kennel and she immediately started to eat. The rest of the dogs were all placed into their pens.

Before leaving the shelter for the night, we made one final check on our newest guests. The momma pit bull and her babies were all nestled in the straw of their warm pen. The other dogs were contently sleeping, having surrendered to the peaceful slumber that comes when you know you're safe. But when we got to Voodoo's kennel, we saw that she had climbed onto the top of her Dogloo and was looking out at the world around her. She had picked up a stuffed bear from her pile of toys and was snuggling it between her giant paws as if it were a little baby. Her big pink tongue was carefully licking the top of the stuffed animal's head. She was the picture of contentment.

Although it had been an exhausting forty-eight hours, it was gratifying to know that we had made a difference in these precious animals' lives. And now that they were entrusted to our care, we would do our best to ensure that their next home was as different in every way possible from their last situation.

CHAPTER 23

Change Is in the Air

■ ■ ■ ■ ■

Photo by Diane Trull

MISTER BLUE

Mister Blue was leaning against a tree when he was found by a local law enforcement agent. Something extremely caustic had been poured over the poor dog's entire body. Only the tip of his nose, his eyes, and the end of his tail were untouched. His condition was so horrific that the officer who found him didn't know what to do, so he called us. We immediately took Mister Blue to the veterinarian.

For two weeks, Mister Blue could only stand in

the corner of his kennel. He was so badly burned he could not lie down, although he had plenty of medication to manage the pain. Slowly, he started healing, physically and emotionally, and was able to leave the clinic after a month. Due to his compromised state, he was in and out of the veterinarian's office for several more months, but he eventually made a full recovery and was ready to go to our weekend adoption events.

One of the managers of a store where we hold our adoptions fell in love with Mister Blue and took him home, where he became part of a loving family.

■ ■ ■ ■ ■

IN 2009, TOUGH TIMES AND BAD WEATHER were abundant. It seemed as if we couldn't get a break. The shelter's struggles seemed to be directly tied to the economy. In general, whenever the economy declines, the number of abandoned animals needing homes increases. And when the economy isn't thriving, we find it that much harder to raise the funds we desperately need to continue our work.

Fortunately, Merrick Pet Care, which has always been so generous to us, continued donating food for all the animals. And since we averaged going through a pallet of dry dog food every day, Merrick's contributions were vital to our existence.

One of our more horrifying surrenders occurred during this time. Mark had picked up some of the children and headed to the shelter early one morning. When he pulled up to the front gate, he saw a large brown mass dangling from the gate.

Mark threw the car into park, ran to the gate, and lifted the dog off the fence. Somebody had left the Newfoundland hooked to the fence with a green coated wire that had become twisted each time the dog had jumped around, eventually shortening its lead. The dog's body was limp, but detecting a weak pulse, Mark started performing CPR and resuscitated the animal. The children named him Brogan.

Katie took Brogan home a few days later, but the cold weather was affecting the dog's arthritis. Although she tried keeping him inside, Brogan was happiest when he was outdoors. We realized he needed to be in a warmer climate and located a rescue group in Phoenix that wanted him. Mark and I drove more than seven hundred miles one way to deliver Brogan to his new foster family. After a few short weeks, the foster family realized they couldn't part with the dog and officially adopted Brogan as their own.

The weather that year was equally challenging. Although the seasons differ widely, the battle in dealing with the varying elements remains constant.

The first week in April, spring was ushered

in by a horrible blizzard. More than two feet of snow fell, creating drifts seven feet tall. Because of the height of the drifts, several dogs were able to climb over the top of their pens and run free outside of the exterior fence. We were constantly corralling them back into their kennels. When we left the shelter on Friday afternoon, the forecast was predicting a winter whiteout. By Saturday morning, the entire sanctuary was cut off.

Late Saturday afternoon, we picked up several of the kids from their homes and headed to the shelter. It took us more than two hours to travel six miles. The snow on the road leading to the shelter was too deep for us to drive, so we parked the truck and walked the rest of the way to the gate.

As we approached the shelter, we could see that the snow had trapped many of the dogs inside their Dogloos. We worked frantically to dig everybody out. The dogs were so happy to see us! Although several of the dogs came down with colds, everyone survived the unexpected spring snowstorm.

The following week, heavy thunderstorms rolled through the area, causing massive mud pools and rivulets throughout the property. A few days after that, we were hit with major windstorms with gusts reaching seventy miles per hour. Despite cement blocks anchoring it down, one of our metal storage sheds blew over and its contents strewn everywhere. The shelter grounds were a total mess.

"This weather is so crazy," Alix announced when she returned to the barn after feeding the dogs one afternoon.

The wind had whipped most of her blonde hair loose from her ponytail. Her knee-high rubber boots were caked in mud. Even though she was a sophomore in high school, Alix still had a girlish charm to her.

"We keep running into so many problems, Mrs. Trull. It reminds me of the children's book *The Little Engine That Could*. We're just like the train in that story. We keep thinking we can save the animals, thinking we can do it, thinking we can do it. And then, finally, somehow, against all the obstacles, we do!"

In the midst of dealing with the wild weather and trying to clean up the aftermath of Mother Nature's wrath, Jesse confided in me that he was leaving Dalhart and moving to Colorado. I was heartsick. I was aware that Jesse was struggling with a lot of things, but I wasn't prepared for his announcement. I offered up a silent prayer that Jesse would be okay and would come back to Dalhart soon.

"I know I should try to talk you out of your decision, but I also know you well enough to realize that it would be pointless," I said.

"I'm sure you're not happy about my leaving,

but I hope you understand, Mrs. Trull," Jesse said. "But please know that no matter where I end up, I want you to know that being at the shelter was one of the few things that always brought me joy."

I reached out and gave him a big hug. I was already missing him.

"You've been such an important part of our work here—it won't be the same without you," I said. "Please promise me you will keep in touch. And if you ever need anything, anything at all, I hope you know that Mr. Trull and I are just a phone call away."

"You don't have to worry about me," he said. "You're one of my heroes, so you won't be getting rid of me that easily."

CHAPTER 24
It Takes a Village

■ ■ ■ ■ ■

Photo by Diane Trull

BOSTON

We found Boston, a brown and white boxer, dumped on the side of the road, close to the sanctuary. When we first approached him, we thought he had been hit by a car. He could barely move, and we rushed him to the veterinarian.

The vet's prognosis was grave. He felt that Boston either had a severe spinal injury or was suffering from a degenerative muscular disease, so he said the best solution, sadly, was to euthanize Boston.

We looked into Boston's eyes and decided we would take him back with us, make him as comfortable as possible, and give him a few days. Cindy, one of our amazing volunteers, took Boston home and showered him with love and attention, along with vitamins and pain medication.

Within a week, Boston was up and walking on his two front legs and gradually putting weight on his back legs. Cindy started massaging his back and within a month he had made a complete recovery.

We took him to an adoption event and a man came who decided Boston needed him, but the man knew he needed his wife's approval before adopting the dog. The man returned with his wife, who instantly fell in love with Boston. By the time the couple was ready to take Boston home, they had already set up a veterinarian/therapist appointment and had purchased a thick orthopedic bed for the long ride home.

Today, Boston is loved and living in a home with two other boxers.

■ ■ ■ ■ ■

WHEN WE FIRST OPENED OUR DOORS in 2003, we had no idea if the shelter would last a month, let alone a year. But after rescuing nearly six thousand precious lives in eight years, it was safe to say that we were committed to animal rescue in Dalhart for the long haul. While I was astonished by those statistics, what I found harder to grasp was the fact that the original group of students who had started the shelter would be graduating from high school within the year.

How could that be possible?

If it wasn't for the children's dedication and desire to literally help the underdog, we would never have taken this journey together. Watching my students blossom into beautiful and mature young adults who understand what it means to be responsible for a life has been a privilege for Mark and me. It was hard to fathom how different our lives would be when they were no longer a daily part of it.

Mark and I came to the startling realization that once the kids were gone, we would be at a crossroads. How would we continue running the shelter? On average, we were caring for six hundred animals every day. Because those numbers had remained constant for a long time, we knew that having extra help from volunteers was critical to our daily operations. We also knew that the most important aspect of working with the community was involving the younger generation in our mission to save animals. Without a doubt, our success has been because of the involvement, dedication, and compassion of so many youth groups.

So when I received a call from one of the administrators at Colorado College wanting to discuss ways in which their students could help us with our work of saving animals, I was thrilled, to say the least. Located in Colorado Springs, Colorado, this liberal arts college sponsors an outdoor education program that enables their students to fan out across the region and spend their school breaks performing a variety of volunteer work. The program builds on the mission of the college by allowing students to enhance their leadership skills, gain a sense of stewardship, and engage in self-discovery through experiential opportunities in the outdoors.

Although it's a four-hour drive from Colorado Springs to Dalhart, the college was eager to partner with us. The first of what would become many groups came during spring break. Instead of heading to a glamorous resort in some exotic destination, eight freshmen and two seniors chose to spend their break at DAWGS and clean pens, walk dogs, shovel out food, pour water, and most important, bestow love on the grateful animals at our shelter. In addition to caring for the daily needs of our rescues, they also assisted with medical care for the sick dogs and reorganized our barn to make it more efficient. This inaugural

272

group of college students stayed with us for ten days. Many came back to volunteer on their own time.

When the group left, Kristin, one of the seniors, adopted Chocolate, a little pit bull mix she "couldn't live without." When she'd first arrived at DAWGS, Kristin told me she couldn't comprehend the concept of caring for hundreds of dogs, but I knew the experience had been a positive one for her when she said what so many other students who visit us during spring break say, "I don't want this week to end."

On our commutes to and from the weekend adoption events in Amarillo, we drive by the entrance to Cal Farley's Boys Ranch. Not knowing much about the organization aside from the fact that it helps children in need, I did a little research and felt it might be a good fit in continuing the legacy of volunteer work that my students had started. The ranch's motto especially resonated with me. "Only through the youth of today is a better tomorrow possible."

The fact that the ranch itself is a thirty-five-minute drive to the shelter was also a plus.

Cal Farley's Boys Ranch is a residential community that helps at-risk children ages five to eighteen. In 1939, Cal Farley, a professional wrestler and Amarillo businessman, accepted a pair of mules, six sheep, a flock of geese, and one hundred twenty acres of land to create a foster home for nine troubled boys. The ranch became a place where boys from broken homes could find, as Mr. Farley put it, "a shirttail to hang on to."

In the late eighties, Cal Farley's Boys Ranch welcomed into its family of services Girlstown, U.S.A., a similar program for girls needing a fresh start. Today, the ranch has morphed into a miniature town with a post office, an activities center, a rodeo ring, twenty-eight homes, and five hundred residents, all revolving around an elementary, middle, and high school.

Since its founding, thousands of children have received nurturing support and structure from the organization. Children who are accepted into the program live in homes with a set of house-parents, attend school, do chores, and participate in extracurricular activities. All of the services are provided at no cost to the children or their families. Because of Cal Farley's generous efforts in helping so many children, he earned the nick-name "America's Greatest Foster Father."

After several meetings with the facility's admin-istrators, we started a pilot program in 2010. Students from the ranch would periodically come to the sanctuary throughout the year and work alongside our regular volunteers. They would help feed the dogs, clean their pens, and provide plenty of play time.

In June, the first group of twenty children came to visit. We spent the better part of that first session educating the children on how to approach the dogs, as well as teaching them the fundamentals of animal behavior. Many of these children had never owned a pet so it was important that we made them feel as comfortable as possible around the dogs.

Once the "official" lesson was over, our new recruits were anxious to walk the dogs and play with the puppies in their pens. My former students were equally eager to help our visitors have a positive experience and show them the ropes. The biggest winners were the dogs. They thrived on the extra attention.

In the midst of all the commotion, Alix was the first to notice that a boy, one of the young visitors from the Cal Farley group, was still standing outside the shelter's entrance. Standing next to him was a middle-aged man waiting patiently. They had not entered with the others.

"Mrs. Trull, do you know why those two haven't come in yet?" Alix asked, nodding her head toward the front gate.

"No, I don't," I said. "Let's go over and see if there's a problem."

At seventeen, Alix had grown into a confident young woman, but she had not outgrown her gentle and caring demeanor.

"Hi, my name is Alix," she said, welcoming

our guests. "We're glad to have you here with us today."

"Hi," the young boy answered. His eyes briefly met Alix's before darting away.

A few seconds of silence passed.

"Do you want to come in and meet any of the dogs?" Alix asked.

More silence.

Finally, the man who was accompanying the boy spoke up. "This is Stephen and my name is Tim, his counselor. Stephen is extremely afraid of animals, especially dogs. He's trying to decide if he wants to go inside the shelter or not."

"Well, we have some really nice dogs here that I think you would enjoy meeting," I said as gently as I could. "And I'm sure they would love to meet you. If you're interested, Alix can introduce you to some of the more quiet ones so it won't be too scary. Just let us know if there's anything we can do to help."

After Tim thanked us for checking on them, Alix and I walked back to where the other students were hanging out.

"I hope that young man can find the courage to step past his fears," I said.

"I know," Alix said. "I can't imagine going through life being afraid of dogs."

For the next hour, Stephen and Tim didn't budge from their spot. From a distance, it was hard to tell if they were talking or just standing in companionable silence. Finally, I happened to look over at the precise moment when the pair started walking slowly through the gate. My heart skipped a beat.

No sooner had they entered when a small boxer named Millie came bursting out of a crowd of several children who had been playing with her. She made a beeline toward Stephen and Tim. Stephen froze, his eyes wide with fear. Once Millie reached them, she threw herself on the ground at Stephen's feet and wriggled her entire body, trying to get him to pet her.

After what seemed like an eternity, Stephen slowly reached down and tentatively started petting her. I watched in amazement, relief, and then delight as Stephen's face broke into a small smile. Before the afternoon was over, Stephen was holding Millie in his arms, carrying her around like a baby.

Tim later told me that Stephen hadn't been able to enter any of the houses at the ranch that had pets living in them. His fear of animals completely immobilized him, so to witness his acceptance of and affection for Millie within a few hours was extraordinary.

By the end of the summer, there were fifty children and their dedicated chaperones making regular visits to the shelter. Although the number of Cal Farley students who participate in our program fluctuates from year to year, our partnership with the ranch gives much-needed socialization to all of our dogs. More important, it helps more children appreciate the value that animals bring to our lives.

CHAPTER 25
To Catch a Thief
■ ■ ■ ■ ■

Photo by Diane Trull

ABBY GRACE

Abby Grace was surrendered to a high-kill shelter in Pampa, Texas, when she was just a puppy. The family that surrendered her had decided a puppy was too much work and they no longer wanted to be bothered. Abby Grace had run out of time when we picked her up.

We took her on our next mobile adoption, and on that same day, Linda came to visit the cute puppies and dogs that were up for adoption. Linda had recently lost her beloved little dog and was hoping someone would catch her eye. After spending time with all the dogs, she saw sweet Abby Grace and knew she was the one.

Linda quickly found that Abby Grace was not only a wonderful companion to her, she was also extremely calm and compassionate to those around her. Linda enrolled Abby Grace in therapy dog training. Within a few months, the dog had learned sign language and was ready to start visiting patients. Abby Grace delights young and old with her tricks, her manners and her sweet kisses and cuddles.

■ ■ ■ ■ ■

DURING THE SUMMER OF 2010, we started noticing that large quantities of dog food were missing from our storage shed. Our biggest expense in running the shelter is purchasing food and since scores of bags were missing on several occasions, it greatly impacted our financial situation.

Merrick was in the process of being sold and had stopped donating food to us temporarily. As a result, we had to purchase our pet food locally, which cost eight hundred dollars for two pallets. We went through one pallet every day in feeding our dogs.

Even more alarming was during that same time frame, we realized that several of our dogs—mostly purebreds and small dogs—were also missing. We felt certain that whomever was taking our food was probably also stealing our dogs. Because we had no idea how the perpetrator was getting into the shelter, we stepped up our security measures.

We posted NO TRESPASSING signs throughout the property, changed the locks on the gates, put metal chains across all the openings, and drove by the shelter at odd hours to check on things. We also questioned everybody associated with the shelter to see if they knew who was behind this. Through one of our volunteers we learned that a local woman named Samantha, who supposedly rescued animals, might have some of our missing dogs.

I had met Samantha on two occasions. The first time I ran into her was at Dollar General when I asked her if she had found my dog, Lucy, who had been missing for several weeks. The second encounter was when Samantha came to the shelter with an employee from Westco Rental to pick up a forklift that we had rented from them. While we were finishing up the paperwork for the rental, she walked around the sanctuary petting our dogs.

Unbelievably, Samantha started telling several people around town, including our volunteer, that she was stealing food and dogs from our sanctuary. Apparently, she had cut off the lock on the back gate and replaced it with a lock of her own. This allowed her to enter the grounds unnoticed between the hours of ten at night and three in the morning.

Luckily, through an informant, we learned exactly when Samantha was planning her next break-in. On August 25th, the night of the planned attack, Mark and Tucker, Katie's husband, in cooperation with the sheriff's department, set up a sting at the shelter and caught Samantha after she had loaded thirty-two bags of our dog food into her car. With the police and Mark standing there, Samantha brazenly claimed she was at the shelter because I had asked her to feed the dogs. She went on to say she had been out there more than thirty times, which explained our huge food loss.

The county arrested her for felony burglary and jokingly referred to it as the "great dog food caper."

After we filed a voluntary statement in which we identified our missing dogs, the police went to her house and found about thirty dogs living in terrible conditions, including five of our missing dogs. Several small dogs were in a one-car garage with dirt flooring covered in feces, and no ventilation, food, or water. Instead of releasing the animals to our care, the judge gave Samantha twenty-four hours to remove all the dogs from the property, including the ones that belonged to us. Because we didn't have much faith that wherever Samantha planned to relocate the dogs would be much better than their current living situation, Katie and I set up a surveillance at her house and watched as several people arrived and loaded up two cars with some of the dogs. We followed the caravan to see where they were taking the dogs, but we lost them on a dirt road.

The next day, we went back to Samantha's house and followed the group again after they loaded up the rest of the dogs. This time we were successful in seeing where they went.

We called the Potter County Sheriff's Department who came and met us there. Unfortunately, the conditions at this second property were no better than the first. There was no food, water, or shade for any of the animals. Eleven small dogs were crammed inside a five-by-five-foot pen and five large dogs were stuffed in a ten-by-ten-foot pen. One of the dogs had just given birth to eleven puppies. After seeing how horrible the conditions were, the police allowed us to remove seven of the dogs.

After posting bond, Samantha was placed on felony probation for stealing dog food from us, which was valued at eleven hundred dollars. She threatened to file charges against me for stealing some of her dogs. She also started making harassing phone calls to our home.

A few weeks later, she moved in down the street from where we lived and started driving by our house daily.

We talked to several lawyers in town about getting a restraining order against Samantha but all three informed us that it would be next to impossible. One of the lawyers, who was also the county attorney, told us that even in spousal abuse cases the odds for getting a restraining order are extremely low.

In September, we filed criminal trespass warnings against Samantha with the Dallam County and Hartley County sheriff's offices. It stopped her from coming around, but her threatening phone calls persisted.

A FEW MONTHS later, I was at the grocery store and spotted Samantha standing in one of the aisles. I immediately turned around and decided to leave. Samantha must have seen me because by the time I reached the front door she came running after me, yelling all sorts of obscenities.

"Your day will come and I'm going to take you down," she screamed.

When I put my hand up to put distance between us, she started screaming, "Don't touch me!"

I walked out of the store and ran into the store manager. I decided I should talk to him about the situation, since it had been quite a scene. As we were talking outside, Samantha marched through the front door and started screaming at me again. I called the police who came and took my statement.

After two weeks, I called the police department to check on the status of the case. They told me that they would not be filing any charges against Samantha. They also told me I could file a citizen's complaint, which I did.

Sadly, nothing ever happened, but I was always watchful for Samantha, especially when I had any of our student volunteers with me.

CHAPTER 26

A Rite of Passage

■ ■ ■ ■ ■

Photo by Diane Trull

CECIL

Cecil was a beautiful border collie–Pyrenees mix that was specially bred in New Mexico to be the ultimate herding dog. Unfortunately, he and his three brothers and sister had zero interest in "minding" the flocks of sheep and goats. Instead, they wanted to run and play all day. When the owner decided he was done trying to train them, he set out coyote traps to catch the dogs, as they would not come to him on their own.

When Cecil and his little sister got caught in the traps, the rest of the siblings stayed with the two dogs to protect them.

The next morning, the man brought us all the dogs. One look at the extent of the dogs' injuries and we knew they needed to see the veterinarian right away. While the little female's leg had to be amputated, the damage to Cecil's leg was less serious, but required months of treatment and rehabilitation.

A year later, we had all the dogs healthy and tame enough to be adopted. We were so happy when they went to their forever homes, leaving Cecil to wait for his turn.

A kind man came to the shelter looking for a dog for himself. He kept going back to Cecil's kennel and asked us if he could take him for a walk. As Cecil came through the kennel gate, he stopped, looked at the man and placed his paw over the man's hand and then collapsed into his arms.

After four years in our care, Cecil finally found his forever home and is greatly loved.

■ ■ ■ ■ ■

IN 2011, WE CELEBRATED two significant milestones. Although both events happened almost simultaneously, one was more bittersweet than the other.

The arrival of spring marked the sanctuary's eight-year anniversary. It was an amazing achievement. So many people had given so much in getting us to that point. I found it serendipitous that we celebrated our five thousandth adoption during the same month as our anniversary.

Earlier in the year, we had received two senior, but adorable, basset hounds named Annie and Spike. They came from a breeder in northeast New Mexico. Since the dogs were past the age to reproduce, the breeder wasn't interested in keeping them, so he surrendered them to us. It was apparent that neither animal had received proper medical care for most of its life.

When Annie and Spike arrived at the sanctuary, they were skinny, sickly, and needy. Spike was also sporting a terrible eye infection. The two dogs came running into the shelter on their squatty little legs and collapsed into our arms.

We immediately took the pair to the veterinarian. Spike was started on a massive dose of antibiotics to try to save his eye. Unfortunately, the trauma his eye endured from lack of care and treatment surpassed the point of being healed with medication. After two weeks, we made the difficult decision to have his eye removed.

Several weeks later, both dogs were spayed and neutered and ready for adoption. Because they had spent their lives together, we had no plans to adopt them out separately. Annie and Spike were a package deal. We were so grateful when a kind man from Pampa, Texas, called and said he wanted to adopt them both after seeing them on our website. It was the happy ending we were hoping for.

The adoption of Spike as our five thousandth adoption happened a few days before several of my former students graduated from Dalhart High School. As Mark and I drove to their graduation ceremony, I couldn't help but reflect on all that we had experienced together.

"I remember feeling this exact same way when Katie and Tyler graduated from high school," I said to Mark, feeling nostalgic. "Graduation is a day of happiness and hope and new beginnings. These kids have their whole futures in front of them. Who knows where they'll end up or what path they will take? And as exciting as all of that is, there's a piece of me that simply wants to keep them close to home and protect them from all the evils of the world."

"Diane, we've done all that we can in helping the kids get to this point," Mark said. "Unfortunately, they have already witnessed some pretty terrible things in their young lives. But they are all well-grounded and resilient and have learned a multitude of life lessons while volunteering at the shelter. I have no doubt they are ready to conquer whatever comes their way."

After the ceremony, we found Alix and Molly talking with a group of their friends. Mark and I gave each of them a hug.

"Mrs. Trull, I can't believe we are officially done with high school," Molly said. A big smile spread across her face. "I never thought this day would come."

"You've had some big moments in your life, but this is definitely one of the biggest," I said. "It was such a privilege for me to be your fourth-grade teacher and I'm grateful that you've been part of our lives ever since. Mr. Trull and I are both so proud of you. What you've accomplished with the shelter is nothing short of amazing. But what makes me the proudest is seeing how each of you has grown into a caring and responsible adult. I know the world is going to be a better place because of you. I love you both."

"Well, we owe so much to you and Mr. Trull," Alix said. "Thanks for always being there for us and for believing in us. You're like a second family to me. You taught us what compassion and loyalty really means. It's going to be weird not going to the shelter every day and seeing you and all the dogs. I'm really going to miss everybody a lot."

"I think this qualifies as a 'tears of happiness' kind of day," Molly said, obviously trying to lighten the moment. "And if anybody starts crying, they better be happy tears!"

CHAPTER 27

Heroes Among Us

■ ■ ■ ■ ■

Photo by Diane Trull

REGGIE

During a severe thunderstorm that blew through Amarillo, one of our volunteers looked out of her window and spotted a small black and white kitten huddled on her front doorstep. Just as the woman opened the door to check on the kitten, a large thunder clap occurred and startled the kitten, who in turn started hissing at the woman. Having worked with feral cats before, the volunteer carefully picked up the kitten and took him inside to safety. She named the cat Reggie.

Within a few months, Reggie was completely tamed and loved being petted. He also loved canned cat food and would "talk and talk" whenever he heard the can opener.

A local family was heartbroken after losing their fifteen-year-old cat and came to one of our adoption events to find a new pet. They saw Reggie from across the room and knew he was the one they needed in their lives.

Today, Reggie adores his new family and loves to find small spaces in which to take a nap. The family said if they can't find him, they simply open a can of food and hear loud meowing as he comes running.

■ ■ ■ ■ ■

THERE WAS A QUIET DESPERATION in the woman's voice on the other end of the line as she explained her situation.

"Hi, my name is Shawnene," she said. "I'm a member of the US Marine Corps and I'm being deployed to Iraq in a few weeks. At the risk of sounding overly dramatic, you might be my last hope."

"Well, if I can help you in any way, I certainly

will," I replied, wondering what I was about to get myself into.

"I live in Arizona with my two cats and they mean the world to me," Shawnene continued. "With my upcoming deployment, there's nobody to care for my pets while I'm gone. Both of my cats have feline leukemia as well as upper respiratory problems that require extra medication and treatment. I've called every rescue group and animal shelter in a five-state radius, but nobody is in a position to help me. I desperately need someone to foster my babies until I return from my tour. Is there any way you might be able to take them for me?"

My heart broke for Shawnene. This brave young woman was fulfilling her duty in serving our country and all she wanted was the peace of mind that her cats would be cared for in her absence. It was hard to believe that nobody was stepping up to help her.

"Let me double check with my husband and see what we can do," I said, not sharing the fact that Mark was severely allergic to cats. "I will call you back tomorrow."

I wondered if Shawnene's cats' diagnoses of feline leukemia was scaring off potential fosters. While feline leukemia is one of the most common infectious diseases among cats, the fact that we didn't own cats anymore was a positive in this instance.

After recounting my conversation with Shawnene to Mark, I asked him the million-dollar question. "Can we do this for her?"

"Where would you keep the cats?" he asked a little hesitantly.

"Well, we can put them in Katie's old bedroom," I said. "We're not using that room for anything right now. And confining the cats to one room should hopefully minimize any problems for you."

Mark and I share a mutual and profound appreciation for our military community. And being the trooper that he is, I wasn't surprised when he agreed that we would foster Shawnene's cats.

Two days later, on New Year's Eve, Mark and I drove ninety-five miles to Tucumcari, New Mexico, where Shawnene met us with her cats, Oscar and Boots. I promised Shawnene that her pets would be safe and well cared for until her return.

"It's absolutely heartbreaking for me to leave them behind," Shawnene said as she absently reached out and scratched behind Boots's ear. "They make such a difference in my life and help me adjust when I come back home. I can't thank you enough for fostering them."

"Mark and I are the ones who should be thanking you for your dedication and service," I said. "We're grateful that we can play a small part in helping you."

We brought the cats safely back to Dalhart and set them up in Katie's bedroom. Oscar was almost feral, which made it practically impossible for me to get near him. Boots was the friendlier of the two, but she suffered from chronic health issues. After Boots had several visits to the veterinarian's office, her condition worsened and she died in my arms a few months after Shawnene's deployment.

I was heartsick at having to tell Shawnene that Boots had passed away, but the veterinarian assured me there was nothing that could have been done to save her. Oscar lived out the year with us until Shawnene safely returned from duty and picked him up.

After caring for Shawnene's cats, Mark and I realized that other military members were probably facing similar challenges in finding someone to care for their pets during their deployment. Thankfully, there's a lot of research that shows people who own pets experience myriad health benefits, from increased physical activity to decreased feelings of loneliness. For service men and women returning from active duty and trying to reintegrate back into civilian life, a pet can be a lifesaving companion. We decided we wanted to help homeless animals find love and companionship with our nation's heroes.

We started a program called Hounds 4 Heroes, which honors the commitments and sacrifices the military community and first responders make for our country. Through the program, we take in pets from people called to duty and care for them while they are away, giving them peace of mind. And for any person returning from duty who doesn't have a pet but is interested in adopting one, we offer discounted adoption fees in gratitude for their dedicated service. We try very hard to match the veterans with pets that are the right fit for their needs and lifestyle. It can really make a difference in their lives.

Like Sheldon did for Roddy.

Roddy came to one of our Amarillo adoption events looking for a pet that needed extra encouragement and care. Roddy had recently returned from his latest tour of duty in Afghanistan, where a bomb had taken his left leg from the knee down. Like many in the military, he was dealing with post-traumatic stress disorder.

When Roddy didn't find the special dog he was hoping for that afternoon, I invited him to come to the shelter and look at the hundreds of dogs living there. I was happy to see Roddy and his girlfriend show up a few days later.

For several hours, Roddy and his girlfriend roamed about the sanctuary visiting all of our rescues. Things got interesting when they stopped in front of Sheldon's cage. Sheldon was an older husky that we had rescued from Amarillo's animal control years ago. He had originally lived indoors with his previous owners until he developed mange due to stress. His owners then moved Sheldon outside, where he was tied to a chain and had little protection from the elements. Sheldon got sunburned on top of the mange, at which point his owners decided they didn't want to care for him any longer and surrendered him to their local animal shelter.

When we rescued Sheldon, he was suffering from extreme skin damage. It took a long time before he was healed and ready for adoption. Complicating his medical issues was the fact that Sheldon was a very large and somewhat intimidating animal. Many people assumed that because of his size Sheldon was possibly aggressive. In reality, the opposite was true. Sheldon was a gentle giant. We were having difficulty finding the right home for him. After six years in our care, we thought Sheldon might be one of the few dogs that would live his entire life at the sanctuary with us.

Sheldon normally stayed inside his Dogloo when potential adopters came to visit, but when Roddy stopped at his kennel, Sheldon ran to the fence. It was an instant connection and we were thrilled when Roddy told us he had found the special dog he had been searching for.

Roddy and his girlfriend managed to squeeze Sheldon into their fire engine–red, two-seater sports car and headed home.

A few weeks later, they brought Sheldon back to one of our adoption events for a visit. Roddy had taught Sheldon to "shake hands," so everyone from the workers in the grooming department to the cashiers at the front registers shook Sheldon's paw.

Not only was it wonderful that Sheldon had found a great home but an added bonus for us was that Roddy started volunteering at DAWGS. From helping at our adoption events to fostering some of our dogs, Roddy became an important part of our community. And although Roddy's relationship with his girlfriend didn't last, Sheldon continues to serve as Roddy's rock by helping to keep him calm, especially during holiday celebrations when fireworks are being set off.

Hounds 4 Heroes is just one more way for us to honor those who give so much. It's a special program that really resonates with me. Special pets for special people.

CHAPTER 28
Aged to Perfection

■ ■ ■ ■ ■

Photo by Diane Trull

BEAUREGARD

Beauregard (aka Beau) was a dog that many
people said was unadoptable. He was found in an
abandoned home in Amarillo. Because he had a
large mass on his chest, he was immediately taken
to a local veterinary clinic for an examination.

Instead of any sort of cancerous growth in his
chest, the veterinarian determined that Beau was
just a big boy and needed to be on a healthy diet.
He was sent to the local animal control facility
where he waited for someone to rescue him, but
sadly no one ever arrived.

When Beau was scheduled to be euthanized,

we took him in. We put Beau on a healthy diet of Merrick grain-free dog food and started taking him on long walks. As his weight slowly came off, he became a much happier dog.

Finally, Beau was able to go to adoptions and through our Silver Paws program, he found a very nice woman who thought he was the most perfect dog ever. The woman had recently moved to a gated community and was very lonely. She was thrilled to have a companion to love.

The woman continued bringing Beau to visit us at our weekend adoption events and spoiled him by buying new toys and healthy treats.

■ ■ ■ ■ ■

S HORTLY AFTER LAUNCHING our Hounds 4 Heroes program, we had a visit from a senior citizen, Helen, who was interested in adopting a dog. Helen's husband had recently passed away. She lived out in the country and was afraid of being alone at night. She decided having a dog around would help solve her problem.

New to the world of pet ownership, Helen thought it might be easier if she adopted a small dog. But fate had other plans for her. By the time she left the shelter a few hours later, her new best friend and personal escort was a one-hundred-pound black Labrador named Big John.

When Helen was filling out the adoption paperwork, we learned that she was living on a fixed income. Because she was a first-time adopter and was grieving the loss of her husband, we decided to discount the adoption fee for her.

The next morning, Cindy and I were talking about Big John's adoption and how happy we were that Helen and Big John had found each other. Seeing how appreciative Helen was when we offered to lower the adoption fee, Cindy suggested that we consider starting a program that helps other senior citizens.

"There's so much research that shows how pets have a positive impact on the elderly," Cindy said. "From lowering blood pressure and pulse rates to offering affection and unconditional love, the comfort and companionship of pets help people live longer. I'm sure there are many senior citizens right here in Dalhart who, at some point in their lives, owned a pet and miss having one around. I think we should find ways to encourage caring senior citizens to adopt animals that need a home."

"That's a great idea, Cindy," I said. "Many senior citizens still live independent lives and would benefit socially, mentally, and physically from having a pet. If an elderly person has given up on the idea of owning a companion animal because of financial concerns, then we should find a way to bridge that gap. And this might be a good way to get more of our senior pets adopted as well."

Sadly, senior pets are often overlooked at animal shelters and adoption events. They can be seen as disposable because potential owners don't think they'll be as much fun as puppies or kittens, or because people are concerned about medical costs as the animal ages. But the magic of senior animals is that they require less work because they have established routines, personalities, and schedules. Although the adoption of senior animals is catching on, there are still countless cats and dogs waiting in shelters that continue to grow older as they get passed over for their younger counterparts.

Cindy's suggestion made me realize that senior citizens are a perfect group for appreciating pets. By making it easier for our area's seniors to adopt pets, their lives could be enriched with joy, love, and lifelong companionship. It was a logical way to ease what's often the most common complaint of the elderly—being lonely.

The next month, Helen stopped by with Big John at one of our adoption events in Amarillo.

"I thought you might like to see how well Big John is doing," Helen said to me. "My plan was to make him a guard dog, but he jumped in bed with me the first night I brought him home. Diane, it was the best night of sleep I ever had!"

After hearing Helen's success story, we started a program called Silver Paws, which promotes the adoption of needy, homeless animals by caring senior citizens. To those seniors over the age of sixty-five who qualify, the program offers a reduced adoption fee and a return policy at any time. We also offer discounted veterinary services and provide assistance with pet food, if needed. And if a senior citizen is also a veteran, we give them the Hounds 4 Heroes and the Silver Paws discounts. We want to make owning a pet for this wonderful group of people as affordable as possible.

One of our first Silver Paws matches was made after Homer and Mary lost their precious dog to cancer. Anxious to get another pet, the senior-citizen couple asked their granddaughter, Maeghan, to help them find another dog. Maeghan suggested they contact us.

A few weeks earlier, we had rescued a little red dachshund named Sassy from a local animal control facility. Although Homer and Mary lived in the Dallas area, they fell in love with Sassy when they saw her photos online. After Sassy was transported to her new home, Homer and Mary called to tell us how perfect she was for them and how much she loves to chase her ball. Because of Sassy, they were taking more walks and enjoying a more active life.

ONE OF THE unexpected joys in maintaining our shelter comes from many of the amazing donors we've met along the way. Jerry and Bertie fell into this category.

Jerry and his lovely wife, Bertie, first heard about DAWGS in 2004 when he came across a small article in the *Best Friends Animal Society* magazine that highlighted DAWGS' larger-than-life efforts in saving homeless animals.

Jerry immediately contacted me, asking about our work and the animals in our care. At seventy-five years young, he decided to drive from Houston to Dalhart, a seven-hundred-mile journey, to see the shelter in person. When he and Bertie arrived, they fell in love with Buddy, a golden retriever–collie mix. Jerry and Bertie had recently lost their golden retriever, Beau, and desperately wanted to find another dog that could share their lives and their home. Once they met Buddy and heard his story, they knew they needed to find a way to get him to Houston.

Buddy was our hero dog. He was one of the first dogs that came into our care and was quickly adopted by a woman named Margaret. The two had a rocky start, but finally became close friends. One day, Margaret was working in her yard and got wedged between her house and the air conditioning unit. Buddy sensed the danger and ran for help, saving Margaret's life. A few months later, though, Margaret decided she wanted to build a pond with ducks on her property. She feared Buddy would disturb the ducks, so she returned him to us.

After visiting our shelter, Jerry went to see his doctor for a checkup and found a kindred soul who loved animals as well. The doctor and his wife offered to fly to Dalhart in their private plane and bring Buddy back for Jerry and Bertie. When they arrived, we asked if they would also take Buddy B, another golden we had rescued that was bound for a golden retriever rescue group in Houston. During the flight home, the doctor and his wife fell in love with Buddy B, and decided to adopt him, giving him a wonderful home.

Jerry and Bertie quickly settled into life with Buddy and would often call us with the latest escapades of "the Bud." After adopting Buddy, Jerry continued to promote several of our dogs and was instrumental in the placement of two more beautiful goldens named Ginger and Tex.

In 2008, Jerry was injured, facing three major brain surgeries, and was very ill. He credited the loving support of his family and his great need to get home to take care of Bertie and Buddy for his remarkable recovery. Through his months of rehabilitation, Jerry never failed to check on the animals at DAWGS to ensure they were all doing well, while minimizing his delicate condition.

Sadly, Jerry passed away in 2012 after a brief illness. It was a great honor to know him, and our lives and the lives of the animals he helped rescue, shelter, and rehome are forever changed. He was truly an amazing man and humanitarian, who unselfishly gave of himself to others. His great kindness and affection for animals and people will be greatly missed by everyone who knew him and loved him.

CHAPTER 29
Charlie's Lucky Break

■ ■ ■ ■ ■

Photo by Diane Trull

ATHENA

We received a phone call from an animal hospital in Amarillo about a dog with a broken leg. The owners wanted to euthanize the dog instead of trying to mend her leg. The clinic asked the owners to surrender the dog instead if a rescue group could be found that would help. The couple agreed, and we went to meet Athena. She weighed less than five pounds and was in terrible pain from her fractured leg.

The veterinarian operated, and we waited six long weeks for the leg to heal. Because Athena needed constant monitoring for the first twenty-four hours after surgery, her foster mom, Debbie, brought her to Petco (our mobile adoption site at the time) to keep an eye on her. A very nice couple saw Athena and asked if she was available for adoption. After they heard her story, the couple wanted to complete an adoption contract in advance, so they could take her home when she healed.

The couple adored the dog and came to our weekly adoptions for six weeks just to spend time with her. When Athena went back to the vet for her medical release, we were devastated to learn that the leg had not healed properly and needed to be amputated. Although Athena had been through so much already, she bounced right back after the operation and felt so much better.

Her adopted parents could not wait to get her home to love and spoil her.

■ ■ ■ ■ ■

ON MOST DAYS, IT SEEMS like my cell phone never stops ringing. And as a result, it's not unusual for me to have thirty to forty voice messages at the end of the day. Some of the calls are from our loyal donors wanting to know if there's anything we need that they can purchase for us. Other calls are from people who want more information about any one of our many dogs available for adoption on the online pet adoption websites. But sadly, most of the messages are from people asking if they can relinquish their pets to us. Their reasons for reaching out are often heartbreaking and a little piece of me dies when I hear each sad tale. We do our best to help as many of these people as possible, but the reality is that most of the time our kennels are overflowing and we simply don't have the capacity to accommodate all the animals in need.

Such was the case with Charlie.

I received a frantic call from a young couple in Amarillo who had rescued a puppy minutes before it was about to be crushed by a garbage truck compactor. The couple had gone for a walk around their apartment complex when they saw a garbage truck pull up to the big metal dumpster in their parking lot. Over the roar of the motor and the crushing of the garbage, they heard muffled barking and whimpering coming from inside the trash bin. They flagged the truck driver and stopped him moments before the dumpster was about to be upended into the back of the truck. That's when they spotted something jumping around on top of the trash pile.

The dumpster was lowered back to the ground, and with the help of the garbage men, the couple pulled out a dark brown, scruffy-looking puppy. Although he was covered in all sorts of debris, the little guy never stopped wagging his tail as he eagerly bestowed kisses on his rescuers. The couple lived in a complex that didn't allow pets so they called and asked if we could help. Our network includes several foster families in the Amarillo area. After a few phone calls, I was able to find someone who agreed to take the puppy.

The foster mom named the dog Charlie and took him to the veterinarian for a checkup and to get his first round of shots. The vet estimated that Charlie was about four months old and was some sort of griffon mix.

Once Charlie received all of his shots, he became a regular celebrity at our adoption events in Amarillo. Although people were touched by his tragic start in life, nobody seemed interested in adopting him. Several weeks had passed and Charlie still hadn't found his forever home.

The following month, I was catching up on my voice mail and discovered that I had received a call from a woman named Bernadette who lived in New York City. She had seen pictures on our website of two sibling dogs named Earl and Sally that were also griffons. In her message, Bernadette explained she had recently lost her beloved griffon and was anxious to adopt another one. She had been searching the animal shelters in the New York region looking for one but without any luck. Bernadette went on to say that her preference was to adopt locally, but since none of the groups in her area had any griffons, she had expanded her search outside New York. DAWGS was the only shelter in the United States that she could find that had griffons available for adoption.

I called Bernadette back but got her voice mail. I explained that Earl and Sally had already been adopted. Their new owner was battling cancer and we weren't sure if the woman would be able to keep the dogs long term, but, at the moment, Earl and Sally were not available. Since this caller had expressed a particular interest in griffons, I mentioned Charlie and asked if she might be interested in adopting him.

The next day, I had another message from the woman saying she would like more information on Charlie. She went on to say that her name was Bernadette Peters and asked that I call her back.

After listening to Bernadette's voice message, I thought it was ironic that she had the same name as the famous actress and singer. When we finally connected, I asked her about her name.

"So, your name really is Bernadette Peters?"

"Yes," the woman said. "I'm Bernadette Peters, the actress."

Not once did it occur to me that the messages

I was getting from Bernadette Peters could possibly be from *the* Bernadette Peters. I was taken aback but thrilled to be speaking with her.

"Oh my," I said, chuckling. "I have to tell you that when my husband and I were first dating, we went on a double date with my cousin and her husband to see your latest movie at the time, *The Jerk*. We stood in line for hours and loved every minute of the show!"

In addition to Bernadette's highly successful professional career, I knew that she was also a passionate animal advocate. In 1999, she cofounded Broadway Barks with her good friend and fellow actress Mary Tyler Moore, who was also an animal lover. Broadway Barks is a charity event held every July in Shubert Alley in the heart of the Broadway theater district in New York City. The program promotes the adoption of homeless animals from New York City animal shelters and rescue groups. Performers and celebrities from the Broadway community introduce the cats and dogs at the annual event.

It was exciting to think that Bernadette might be interested in one of our rescues.

After our conversation, I sent Bernadette a picture of Charlie, followed by a video that I took of him. Within a few days, she called to tell me that she and her assistant were flying to Amarillo to meet Charlie. I picked the dog up from his foster family and went to the hotel where

Bernadette was staying. As soon as we got out of the car, Charlie ran over to Bernadette and gave her a big kiss. We spent the next hour walking Charlie around the hotel parking lot while I gave Bernadette as much background information as I could about him.

"I'd like to keep Charlie overnight," Bernadette said. "I've got another dog back home and I want to be sure that his personality and temperament will be a good fit with Stella's."

"That would be great," I said. "As you can see, Charlie is a wonderful, goofy dog and I don't think you'll have any problems with him."

The next morning, Bernadette told me the good news—she wanted to adopt Charlie. Her assistant had already arranged to rent a van so they could drive Charlie back to New York City.

Once they returned home, Bernadette called and told me how well Charlie had done on the trip and that he and Stella, her pit bull, were getting along just fine.

In fact, Charlie settled into his new life so well that he was featured in a children's book. Bernadette wrote a series of books inspired by her own pets to help support Broadway Barks. *Stella and Charlie, Friends Forever* tells of Charlie's rescue and how he learned to get along with Bernadette's older dog, Stella, while teaching valuable lessons about love and sharing.

My biggest hope for all our rescues is that they

find their perfect forever home. Bernadette's adoption of Charlie was far greater than anything I could have imagined for him. His story brings new meaning to the phrase that one person's trash is another person's treasure.

CHAPTER 30

The Journey Continues

■ ■ ■ ■ ■

Photo by Diane Trull

MAX AND BONNIE

Max and Bonnie were two-year-old German shepherds who lived in Lubbock, Texas. Their former family decided to stop feeding them to see how long they would survive.

Fortunately, a neighbor saw what was happening and contacted the authorities.

Lori, one of our marvelous fosters, closely followed the story. When the dogs were available to be fostered, she picked them up and immediately took them to the veterinarian. Both dogs were about thirty pounds underweight and had multiple health issues.

After several months of expensive treatments, Bonnie went to her forever home where she has a new best friend, Nitro. Max experienced some setbacks but within a few months after Bonnie's adoption, he, too found his forever home.

■ ■ ■ ■ ■

GREEK PHILOSOPHER HERACLITUS IS credited with saying, "The only thing constant is change." Without a doubt, life at the shelter has undergone a lot of change. But change can be good and we've learned to embrace all that comes our way.

But one of our saddest moments came in 2015 when we had to say good-bye to Hooch, the dog patriarch of our shelter. Hooch and Cheyenne had arrived within a few days of each other when we first opened our doors in 2003. Back then, both were convalescing from severe injuries and illnesses and spent long hours napping together. Over time, the pair became inseparable. Because of their strong bond, we tried for years to find them a home together, but we were unsuccessful. So, while Hooch and Cheyenne patiently waited for their forever home, they became our official greeters at the shelter, sharing a kennel by the front gate. Even after Cheyenne's tail was amputated and the two dogs could no longer wrap their tails together, they would always walk side by side, the sides of their bodies touching.

When Hooch was diagnosed with cancer, it broke our hearts. We made the decision to euthanize him in the kennel with Cheyenne present, so she could say good-bye to him. We buried Hooch underneath the sanctuary sign at the front of our property and every spring I sprinkle wildflower seeds in the area where he is buried. Letting Hooch go was one of the hardest things we ever had to do.

After Hooch's passing, Cheyenne became very depressed and stopped eating. A nice family in town heard about what had happened between the two friends. They rushed out to the shelter and adopted her on the spot. Cheyenne had a tough few days but settled into her new life with her wonderful family. She lived out the rest of her years hanging out in their kitchen and snuggling on soft pillows.

REGARDLESS OF THE trials and tribulations, we remain steadfast in our pursuit of getting our dogs and cats into loving and forever homes as well as teaching compassion and caring to people of all ages.

Because we have established relationships with several shelters and rescue groups outside of Texas, we regularly transport our puppies and dogs to Colorado, Missouri, New York, and Pennsylvania. It's hard to fathom, but some parts of the country have a shortage of adoptable dogs. We needed a large van to facilitate the transports and turned to an amazing donor, Leslie. She provided the funds for a transport van in memory of her sweet Sydney, an adorable silky terrier. Most of the animals we send find homes within weeks of arriving at their new destinations. Some are even adopted before they leave Dalhart. We had several black Labrador puppies we had been trying to get adopted for almost a year. Every weekend, we took them to our adoption events, but we were unable to place them in loving homes. We sent the puppies on a transport to Denver, and within one hour of their arrival, they were all adopted.

With the help of our tremendous donors, especially Leslie, Wendy, Janet, Nancy, and Karen, we built a new twenty-four-foot by eighty-foot enclosed building that houses our adoption center and puppy play area. We also built four hundred feet of covered space extending on each side of the building, which allowed us to relocate many of the kennels. The majority of our dogs are now protected from the direct sun and we no longer have to hang shade tarps over the kennels for shade in the summer. More important, it means the dogs are more accessible to our visitors. For our volunteers and helpers, the improved layout reduces the time needed to feed and water the dogs and clean their pens. This allows us to spend more time socializing with each animal, which improves their adoptability.

Weather permitting, we still head south to Amarillo most weekends for our adoption events. For several months, we held simultaneous events at both PetSmart and Petco to provide more opportunities for the adoption of our wonderful cats and dogs. (At one point, we ranked as high as number nine in Petco's adoptions nationwide and number four in Petco's adoptions in the region.) But trying to coordinate drivers, volunteers, and animals for two stores was getting complicated so we opted to hold our events at the PetSmart location only, as they had so much more space.

We've also become more environmentally conscious and started composting our animal waste with used hay. Additionally, we started recycling our dog food cans and bags. We do our best to reduce our ecological footprint and help the environment.

We continue to rely on our wonderful volunteers, who make a difference each day with their love for the animals and their desire to help. In contrast to all the children who spend time with us, local Dalhart resident Mary Ann earned the title of being our most senior volunteer. At eighty-one years young, Mary Ann faithfully came to the shelter every Sunday and brought treats for the animals. She had a soft spot for collies and adopted several from us over the years. After her last rescue passed away, she decided she was too old to get another dog. A stray cat that had been wandering in her neighborhood for months decided to take up residence at Mary Ann's house. Mary Ann took the cat in and named him Mr. Mac. They became perfect companions, proving that animals don't care about a person's age.

Although we've accomplished a lot since our early days, Mark and I still have big plans for the sanctuary. Our dream is to build an onsite spay-neuter-and-wellness clinic that will provide a low-cost sterilization program for the surrounding communities. We also hope to build a natural windbreak out of trees to protect the shelter from the forces of nature that regularly occur in the Texas Panhandle. The expanded facilities would enable us to continue giving second chances to hundreds of homeless dogs while teaching community awareness, responsibility, and commitment to scores of young people who volunteer at the shelter.

Looking back on that historic day when my class earnestly inquired about saving homeless dogs, nobody could have predicted that the students would soon become the teachers. Through their selfless actions, a group of elementary school-age children taught a community an important lesson: we can all make a difference. And when those actions stem from the heart, love really can work miracles.

Afterword

BY MEREDITH WARGO

I FIRST LEARNED about the Dalhart Animal Wellness Group and Sanctuary in 2004, after reading about their efforts in the *Best Friends Animal Society* magazine. Although I was touched by the heartwarming tale, I remember having some reservations about the story. It's nice to think that children could create a no-kill world for the strays in their area, but, even though I'm not a cynic, logic told me that the odds of a group of elementary school-age children successfully running a shelter were probably low.

My curiosity remained piqued, though, long after reading the article. I started following the group on their social media sites and learned more about what they were trying to accomplish. Although they were facing unprecedented odds from Mother Nature and their community, the group seemed focused on their mission. The more I learned, the more I was impressed with their unusual model, as well as their dedication.

My relationship with DAWGS officially began when I sent them a small donation and received a handwritten thank-you note from cofounder Diane Trull in return. In our increasingly digital and remote world, Diane's choice to send a personalized note spoke volumes about her character.

Over the next two years, Diane and I started a long-distance friendship. I continued sending donations and Diane continued penning her heartfelt thank-you notes. It was through this exchange that I got a glimpse of what life was like at DAWGS. I shared in their sorrows when they were confronted by myriad challenges and celebrated their triumphs, no matter the size.

Although I lived seven hundred miles away from Dalhart at the time, I felt connected to their cause and wanted to somehow help the group. I offered to donate my freelance services and write an article about the sanctuary in the hope of gaining some publicity and support for what they were doing. Diane graciously accepted.

Never having traveled to the Texas Panhandle before, I eagerly planned a trip to Dalhart to interview the kids, Mark, and Diane, as well as get an inside look at what it's really like to manage a shelter that houses hundreds of animals. I remember having some trepidation prior to my trip because the rubber was about to meet the road.

What if the shelter wasn't anything like how it's portrayed on their website? What if the animals weren't being properly cared for? What if the children weren't really involved in caring for the animals? What if, what if, what if...

Fortunately, all my fears were allayed shortly after my arrival. The facilities were clean, the animals were well cared for, Diane and Mark were as genuine and down-to-earth as I believed them to be, and the children were the driving energy behind the shelter. It was easy to see that everyone's love for the animals permeated every aspect of the sanctuary.

It's no secret that homeless animals abound in every community—large and small, urban and rural. And for most shelters, the problems and struggles are real and ongoing. In that regard, DAWGS is no different from any other shelter. There are always too many animals in need of homes and not enough funds to care for the ones that are lucky enough to find temporary sanctuary with a rescue group.

Sadly, more than two thousand, two hundred dogs and cats are put to death every single day in America's shelters because there are simply not enough homes for them. Each of these animals is an individual, a life worth saving. Although the number of homeless animals varies by state, the majority of animals euthanized in shelters are the offspring of accidental litters.

So, what is the solution to preventing unwanted births and ensuring that animals don't have to face a lonely and heartbreaking death?

Spaying and neutering.

It's a passionate topic among those involved in animal welfare, including state, city, and local jurisdictions, veterinary associations, advocates, and pet lovers. Most groups agree that something needs to be done to curb the homeless animal overpopulation. And most agree that community awareness and education—not more laws—will address the root problem of the crisis.

Fortunately, the spay-neuter movement is gaining traction. And as it grows, so does the availability of affordable resources. There are numerous initiatives that provide low-cost or free spay and neuter services throughout the country. While many of these services are for low-income families or senior citizens, there is ample help available for anybody who is interested in getting their pets fixed.

That's why Mark and Diane's dedication to promoting spay-neuter awareness throughout their community is spot-on and commendable. It's the only viable means of curbing animal homelessness while lessening the burden on shelters and rescue groups in caring for these animals.

It's simple arithmetic. When intake numbers are reduced, shelters have more resources to create programs that aren't possible when they are overwhelmed caring for too many animals. Instead of spending their limited funds on euthanasia, they can focus on training and rehabilitating the animals in their care, which greatly improves the animals' chances of being adopted.

But even if intake numbers drop, shelters and rescue groups can only do so much by themselves. Most of the work done to save animals takes place out of the kindness and generosity of like-minded people who band together.

The good thing is, there is always something—big or small—that each of us can do to help homeless animals. Volunteer an hour a week at your local shelter to walk the dogs or read to the cats. Use your knowledge and skills as a lawyer or an accountant to help administrators at shelters stay on top of legal forms, contracts, and donations. If you're a social media whizz, spread the word about the adoptable pets in your area on Facebook, Twitter, Pinterest, or any of the other myriad social media platforms. Open up your home and foster an animal for a few days or weeks, or volunteer to transport a dog from the shelter to its veterinarian appointments.

Rescue work is a labor of love. Don't let what you can't do interfere with what you can do. Every small and not-so-random act can make a huge difference to these animals as they wait for their forever homes.

Such was the case on that momentous day when Diane's students asked one seemingly innocent question. At the time, nobody could predict the impact of their concern. But by daring to dream big and doing their small part each and every day, a handful of kids forever changed the lives of thousands of people and animals.

For years, the Trull family was the glue that held all things DAWGS together. As a nonprofit organization, the shelter receives no local, state, or federal aid. All donations go directly to the care of the animals because Mark and Diane personally cover all the administrative duties of running the facility. Throughout the years, the Trulls have tirelessly devoted their lives to saving animals and teaching children and adults the importance of compassion and community service.

Diane and Mark's story is one for the books. Mark proposed to Diane one month after they met. They married in 1980 and began their family in 1983. Mark felt that life was a challenge and that you had to meet it each day. He was known for often saying, "Put on your boots, take one step and then another, and carry on."

And then in 2017 the unthinkable happened. Mark was diagnosed with Stage 4 cancer and passed away on September 17, 2017.

During the course of writing this book, Diane often shared with me her desire to include more personal stories about Mark. Although he loved animals, his love for her was the reason he put up with the constant barrage of issues that surrounded the sanctuary. But because Mark didn't feel comfortable being in the limelight, Diane honored his feelings.

As a way to pay tribute to Mark's legacy, I believe it's only fitting to include my favorite story that Diane shared with me about their relationship. In Diane's words:

One day, there had been a horrible blizzard. It was too cold for the kids to go out and care for the dogs, so it was just Mark and me. The game plan was that we would start at opposite ends of the shelter and each of us would feed half of the animals and meet in the middle. At the time, we had about six hundred dogs in our care. It was close to midnight when I came around the corner wondering how close Mark was to being finished. It was bitterly cold, and we were both worn out from working all day. There was a ten-foot-high chain-link fence around the shelter and it was blanketed in snow. In between feeding his portion of the animals, Mark had taken the end of a broom handle and carved out the words "I love you, Mrs. Trull" in big letters on the snow-covered fence. He was a wonderful man and I love him so much!

Although Mark, Katie, Tyler, and countless others selflessly contributed to DAWGS' success over the years, Diane is the heart and soul of the shelter. Standing at five-foot-six, she is not to be underestimated or overlooked. Her gentleness and soft voice bely her strength and determination to protect every child and animal in her care. Diane is genuinely kind, empathetic, trustworthy, and loyal. Time and time again she gives others the benefit of the doubt. While kudos and compliments make her feel uncomfortable, she is quick to point out the achievements of those around her. Without a doubt, her modesty is her most endearing trait. Diane's unwavering dedication to creating a sanctuary in an unlikely and inhospitable location gives hope and inspiration to countless others who continually fight for the rights of innocent homeless animals across the country.

Since its founding in 2003, DAWGS has touched the lives of more than twenty thousand animals, giving them a second chance in life. Their story has been—and continues to be—a tale of conviction, dedication, compassion, and triumph.

As cultural anthropologist Margaret Mead said, "Never doubt that a small group of thoughtful, committed citizens can change the world; indeed, it's the only thing that ever has."

Acknowledgments

THE DICTIONARY DEFINES thank you as "a polite expression of one's gratitude." After reading that definition, I'm not sure how those two little words will adequately convey my feelings and appreciation toward all the people who have so generously supported DAWGS throughout the years.

At the beginning of this journey, our focus was simply to help as many animals as possible make it into their forever homes. What we didn't expect was the outpouring of goodness and kindness from countless people who shared our passion.

Every donation that we have ever received—no matter the amount—has meant the world to us. From the senior citizens who faithfully send us ten-dollar checks every month along with a handwritten note to those individuals who, without batting an eye, answer our frantic pleas for help whenever we face major expenses in running the shelter, it all matters. We couldn't have achieved what we've accomplished if it weren't for the generous benevolence of our loyal supporters and donors.

And although many of you were total strangers in the beginning, you have become trusted and cherished friends over the years. It's an honor to have you in the DAWGS family.

So, to each of you who has lovingly supported our cause with donations, adoptions, words of encouragement, or outpouring of love, my most humble and heartfelt thank you.

—Diane

Writing this book has long been a dream of mine. There have been so many people who have traveled this amazing journey with me. I am grateful to my husband, Tom Langley, my brother, Mark Wargo, and my dearest friend, Jane Goodsill, for your endless encouragement and support. My love and thanks.

I would also like to thank Michaela Hamilton and the entire team at Kensington, who share a love for animals and whose deep affection for this story was evident from the very beginning.

Lastly, I would like to thank the Trull family— Mark, Diane, Katie and Tyler—for their dedication, compassion, and devotion in helping countless number of animals find new homes throughout the years. There would be no story at all if not for your tireless acts of love that have inspired so many.

My hope is that *DAWGS* will be a lasting testament to all those involved in animal rescue, no matter how young or old.

—Meredith

Volunteers snuggle with their favorite puppies. *Photo © 2019 Karen Kuehn.*

Kali, Ally, Molly and Kelsey at the IDA gala.

Mark and several volunteers making the holidays merry!

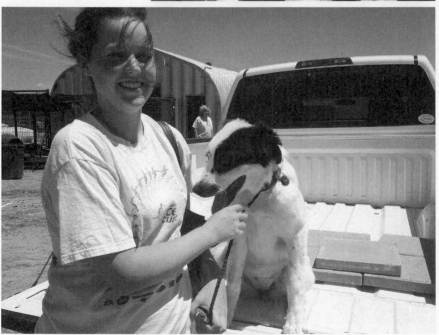

Maegan with her newly adopted dog, Gracie.

Katie and Tucker at PetSmart on adoption day.

Volunteers assist with food preparation and feeding. *Photos © 2019 Karen Kuehn.*

Photo © 2019 Karen Kuehn.

Kali, Ally and Molly.

Katie, Jamie, Molly, Sarah and Cortney.
Photo © 2019 Karen Kuehn.

Kat.

Thank you for helping us to make a difference.

One animal at a time,

One child at a time,

One day at a time.

The children show their appreciation to the donors.

THANK YOU

Sophia and Spencer.

Jesse and Fawney.

Hannah and Avery.

Alix and
Chico.

Hannah and Sissy.

Puppy wranglers Olivia and Serenity.

Diane. *Photo © 2019 Karen Kuehn.*

Protecting the hay. *Photo © 2019 Karen Kuehn.*

Katie. *Photo © 2019 Karen Kuehn.*

Kat tending to some of the dogs.
Photo © 2019 Karen Kuehn.

Photo © 2019 Karen Kuehn.

Cheyenne and Hooch.

Angela is ready for the movies!

Photo © 2019 Karen Kuehn.

Diane. *Photo © 2019 Karen Kuehn.*

Katie and Mark sharing a moment.
Photo © 2019 Karen Kuehn.

Setting up pens. *Photo © 2019 Karen Kuehn.*

Cindy getting some love! *Photo © 2019 Karen Kuehn.*

Diane and Mark administering medicine to Hooch.
Photo © 2019 Karen Kuehn.

Mark and Diane. *Photo © 2019 Karen Kuehn.*

Books are produced in the United States using U.S.-based materials	Books are printed using a revolutionary new process called THINKtech™ that lowers energy usage by 70% and increases overall quality	Books are durable and flexible because of Smyth-sewing	Paper is sourced using environmentally responsible foresting methods and the paper is acid-free

Center Point Large Print

600 Brooks Road / PO Box 1
Thorndike, ME 04986-0001 USA

(207) 568-3717

US & Canada:
1 800 929-9108
www.centerpointlargeprint.com